To Ghana with Love

the story of my life

Barbara Baddoo

Copyright © 2008 - 2012 by Barbara M. Baddoo

All rights reserved,

including the right of reproduction

in whole or in part in any form.

Third Edition, 2012

ISBN 978-1-4452-6000-6

Typeset in Garamond and Arial by Jim Baddoo

Line drawings by Janet Price

Cover photo – University of Ghana, Legon - by Kweku Hutchful

Printed by www.lulu.com

Table of Contents

Chapter 1	Beginnings	21
Chapter 2	Schooldays	33
Chapter 3	Meeting Michael at University	49
Chapter 4	A Year in Nigeria	59
Chapter 5	Marriage and Motherhood	71
Chapter 6	Life in a New Culture	85
Chapter 7	Difficult Days	95
Chapter 8	Two Very Different Furloughs	107
Chapter 9	The Gold Coast Becomes Independent	119
Chapter 10	Life at Korle Bu	133
Chapter 11	Busy with Our Five Children	145
Chapter 12	Back to Accra	159
Chapter 13	Michael Retires	171
Chapter 14	The Younger Generation Leave Home	187
Chapter 15	Dronfield Days	205
Chapter 16	Back to Ghana to Face Bereavement	221
Chapter 17	Return to My Roots	233
Appendix A	Herode Kpokpo	245

Photos

Mum and Dad on honeymoon..22
Myself aged four...24
Winifred, Beatrice, my grandmother, Edith and Kitty................27
Jean, myself, Doreen and Peter circa 1928...............................29
Miss Hilda Dodd, Miss Chislett and Miss Annie E Irwin Dodd...30
Myself and Joyce, 50 years later in Derbyshire.........................34
Grovelands Park..35
Jean..41
Missionary Conference - Mrs Rattenbury third from left............46
Scafell Pike - myself second from right with Doreen.................51
Myself..52
Dad..54
Mail Boat - Apapa..60
Michael's father, Peter...63
Michael's mother, Sybilla...64
Our wedding day...75
Uncle Fred, myself, Mum, Rosemary, Michael and Auntie Edie...77
Our first car...81
Flora..86
Theatre nurses with Michael...90
My class in Tamale..91
Henry, Ade and Rosemary...99
Henry and Michael...101
The interpreter, Michael, Rosemary and myself......................104
Pounding fufu..108
Michael examining a leprosy patient.......................................110
Pauline Davey with Henry fast asleep......................................111
The Tarkwa Methodist Church Choir.......................................114
Rosemary, Henry and Winifred..116
Yaro and the children..121
Michael, myself and the children..123
Pamela Hughes, Michael, myself and students......................124
A party at the Larteys, with Doris holding Karley....................125
Silas and Joan Dodu, with Densua and Namua......................127

Clare Parker, Winifred, Michele Amonoo, Karley and Carmen Amonoo	136
Winifred, the future paediatrician, with Jimmy	144
The five children	150
Nurses at the NTC	151
Nursing tutors including Kay Dier (centre)	153
Winifred, Karley and Henry in Ho	155
Sunday afternoon guests – Ann (nee Parker) and Steve far left	161
Winifred with Doreen and Tom Page	163
My mother in her younger days	167
Michael, Henry, Ben Tettey and I	172
Staff at the Institute of Adult Education, Legon	174
Alan and Betty Saunders	177
Lily	179
Wesley Church	182
Sir Geoffrey Keynes and Jim	191
Marion at 'Service to Sport' award	198
Jim's graduation in 1986	202
Michael playing an organ in Sheffield	207
Kweku, Ato, Karley and Kwesi - 1991	211
Ralph, Ayeley, Yoki, Kai, Rosemary and Niiayitey - 1993	212
Myself and Nora	214
Winifred, Almaz, Samuel, Annabel and Yolanda - 2003	216
Henry, Leonora, Rachel, Ruth and Shevon - 1994	217
Kate, Peter, Harriet, Nancy and Jim - 1998	218
Ruby Wedding celebration	222
Michael's grave with Henry, Karley, myself and Rosemary	226
Myself by the white bougainvillea bush	232
My brother Peter	236
My sister Doreen	237
Myself in Reading	239
Michael and I	243

Maps

Map of Ghana..19
Mail Boat Route to West Africa...61
Route from Lagos to Takoradi..68
Journey to Work, 4th June 1979..184

"You can play a tune of sorts on the white keys, and you can play a tune of sorts on the black keys, but for real harmony you must use both the black and the white."

James Emman Kwegyir Aggrey

(1875 - 1927)

Dedicated to my dearly beloved husband

Dr Michael Allotey Baddoo

and to all the good people of the world who demonstrate

"That best portion of a good man's life,

His little, nameless, unremembered acts

of kindness and of love."

William Wordsworth

(1770 - 1850)

Acknowledgements

I should like to thank all those family and friends who have helped create this book, through inspiration, encouragement, editorial advice, factual corrections, photos, line drawings and so on – you know who you are! I am particularly indebted to Kay Dier for inspiring me to complete the task.

As I update the book for the third edition, I am grateful to those who have provided me with some factual corrections which I have endeavoured to incorporate.

This book was mainly written for family and friends. It has therefore been a pleasant surprise to receive some encouraging feedback from people outside this immediate circle, but of course part of our worldwide family.

Barbara Baddoo

January 2012

Map of Ghana

~ *Chapter 1* ~

Beginnings

I was born in April 1924 at 41, Eaton Park Road, Palmers Green in North London. At the time of my birth my mother, Winifred Bain, was 28 and my father, Arthur Bain, was 42. He had lost his first wife, Charlotte (nee Steven), in childbirth with her second child. He was heartbroken, but about ten years later fell in love with my mother and married her. So when I was born, I had an eighteen-year-old half-sister, Lily, a fifteen-year-old half-brother Ken, two older sisters, Doreen, three, and Jean, nearly two. All my mother's babies were born at home under the care of a 'monthly nurse' who came when labour started, delivered the baby, and stayed on as a member of the household until the baby was a month old. I think my mother always had the same 'nurse' (trained midwife really) who became a familiar figure. Three and a half years after my birth, my mother had her last child, Peter, which pleased everyone as she had a boy at last.

Mum was never a very strong woman, so after having three children so quickly she was exhausted. Lily willingly helped to look after me as the new baby, becoming almost like a second mother. She suffered a lot from asthma, missed a lot of schooling, was never considered fit enough to go out to work, and never married. Of course these days she would probably have received more treatment and lived a more normal life.

Mum and Dad on honeymoon

After my father's first wife died, his sister, Mary, lived with him looking after Lily and the newborn baby Ken. Of course when my father remarried it was rather a difficult situation. Looking back, I admire the way my mother (then only twenty-three herself) coped with a fifteen-year-old stepdaughter and a twelve-year-old stepson, as well as a rather austere sister-in-law. We somehow got the impression that Aunt Mary secretly considered that her brother was being disloyal to his first wife's memory by marrying again - even after almost ten years of being a widower! Maybe she thought Mum was too young, as she was fourteen years younger than Dad.

We all lived together in a big house in Elm Park Road. There was a tremendous amount of shopping, cooking and washing-up to do. Every morning in the winter after the ashes from the previous day's fire had been carried outside, a fresh fire had to be lit using screwed up paper, sticks of firewood and small pieces of coal. This was quite an art, and until the fire was blazing, the house would be exceedingly cold. There were no washing machines, so the weekly wash would be done on Monday (taking all day!) and the ironing on Tuesday. Every day the beds would be made (no duvets), the floors swept and the furniture dusted.

All this kept my mother, Lily, Aunt Mary and a daily maid busy from morning till night. Because the coal fires caused so much dust, the annual 'spring-cleaning' of each room was a real necessity. In the winter, we children were regularly ill with childhood diseases like whooping cough, measles and mumps, coughs and colds, and sternly told to stay in bed where it was warm. This meant innumerable trays of food going up the stairs.

Myself aged four

There came a time - presumably because Aunt Mary and my mother didn't 'get on' - when we could no longer all live together. Something had to be done quickly. My father sold the house in Elm Park Road and bought a small house in Green Dragon Lane where Aunt Mary set up house with Ken. The rest of us moved temporarily to a rented house (also in Green Dragon Lane) while my father looked for a more suitable house to buy. The house we went to was (according to my older sister) in a very bad state, needing a good clean and even had some old bacon left in a dirty frying pan!

I was oblivious to all the tension of this unhappy episode. I simply remember that Mr Buckingham (one of my father's partners) and his wife came to visit us just before Christmas bringing us some beautiful dolls! They must have known that my mother was very upset and came to give moral support. We did not stay in this house very long before moving to a beautiful house in Downes Court - but more of that in chapter two.

My father must have been quite prosperous for those days to support two households. He was a very hard-working and successful butcher. He left school at the age of twelve without much formal education, probably starting off as an errand boy, gradually working his way up to assistant butcher, manager of someone else's shop, and then finally owning his own shop at Clapham where he was living when he lost his first wife, Charlotte. He went into partnership for a time with Mr Buckingham and Mr Buttery: together they acquired a number of butcher's shops in both North and South London. After some years they divided the shops between them. My father was allocated the shops in the area around Winchmore Hill, eventually having seven shops. The most important one on the Broadway was always called 'The No 1 Shop'.

I know I greatly admired him because every afternoon he would phone the managers of the seven shops to find out what they needed for the next day. Of course there was little or no refrigeration in those days. He would write the orders down in his own sort of shorthand and the next morning in the early hours would make his way to Smithfield Market in the centre of London, and pick out the best cuts of meat or carcasses. These would be delivered that morning in time for his customers to buy and enjoy for lunch or the evening meal. He also believed in the importance of making good sausages! He knew that people would go a long way to buy tasty sausages, and then buy the meat as well.

As Dad knew the names of many of his customers, I was proud to walk beside him round Winchmore Hill. When these ladies met and greeted him by name, he also would lift his hat, bow slightly and respond politely, 'Good-day, Mrs …'. After they had passed, Dad and I would exchange a look without saying a word. As he didn't have a car at that time, I suppose he went to Smithfield every morning on the train, and walked everywhere when going about his business in Winchmore Hill. He was a familiar figure, well liked by other businessmen, and he got on well with those who worked for him.

Mum came from a large family, the youngest of ten children. I remember her mother Marian, (after whom I was named) very well but her father, Alfred Randall, must have died before I was born. My mother kept up with three of her sisters, Auntie Kitty, Auntie Beattie, Auntie Edie, who all met regularly for tea at each other's houses. My mother went to great lengths when they were due to come to her house. I think she felt she had to prove that even though she was the youngest she could put on a really good 'high tea' with a spotless white cloth, very thin bread and butter, and home made scones and cakes. We three girls sat quietly listening to their fascinating conversation and news about the rest of the family and neighbours. Sometimes they forgot about our presence and strayed into forbidden topics like sex and mental illness. After a few minutes my mother would say sharply, 'Now, children, why don't you go and play in the garden!' We reluctantly disappeared.

Winifred, Beatrice, my grandmother, Edith and Kitty

Dad also came from a large family, and was the youngest of ten children, but he was too busy with his butcher's shops to keep up with them. Aunt Mary visited her older sister Christiana (Aunt Teena) who had a farm at Chertsey, just outside London, and occasionally we heard of Uncle Bob who married Aunt Rose, but that was all. Like many families, we were closer to our Mum's family, especially her sisters, than our Dad's.

Maybe we were considered to be quite an unusual family, because at that time 'family planning' (or 'birth control') was available, and this caused a swing of the pendulum from very large families to very small ones. Many of my friends were only children or had only one brother or sister. When we were living at Elm Park Lane, before my father settled Aunt Mary in her own house with Ken, there must have been nine of us under the same roof - and ten when the 'monthly nurse' was around.

But it was a happy life being a member of such a large family. We didn't have many toys, nor can I remember ever having a birthday party, but we did have bicycles, skipping ropes and balls to throw around. We made up our own games, and played board games like 'Ludo' and 'Snakes and Ladders' and simple card games like 'Snap' and 'Beggar Your Neighbour'. As there were always plenty of people around, I don't remember that we ever complained about being 'bored'. I hero-worshipped Ken and loved it when he called me 'Twinkletoes'. He was so strong and handsome, always active, playing football and tennis. I thought he was wonderful!

As Dad had not had much education himself, he thought he would be giving us a better chance in life by sending us to private schools where fees had to be paid instead of to the state schools

Jean, myself, Doreen and Peter circa 1928

that were free (at least at the primary level). My sisters were at Palmers Green High School, but I went to Winchmore Hill High School, run by three very kind but strait-laced spinsters (as unmarried ladies were called in those days). They were Miss Chislett, Miss Hilda Dodd, and Miss Annie E. Irwin Dodd. They all wore those old-fashioned shoes with a row of buttons at the side, which fascinated me as a young child. The two Miss Dodds lived with their father who could recite from memory the whole of Milton's 'Paradise Lost'. What a feat of memory! This famous long epic poem consists of twelve books, which together total more than 10,000 lines of poetry in blank verse. As Mr Dodd grew older, he recited the whole poem once a year taking all day to do so. The pupils at the school were always told when this was going to take place, and went around the school on that day rather subdued and impressed.

Miss Hilda Dodd, Miss Chislett and Miss Annie E Irwin Dodd

In those days great emphasis was laid on the virtues of obedience, honesty and truthfulness. I remember one incident when I was ten or eleven. Walking along the road I saw a ten-shilling-note lying on the pavement. I picked it up and greatly excited took it home. Lily pointed out that it might be someone's old age pension for the week and the person who dropped it might be very upset. One could buy a lot for ten shillings in those days (50p in today's money). On her advice I took it to the police station and reported what had happened to the rather surprised policeman on duty. He wrote everything down in a large book, told me to come back in a month's time and if no one had claimed it, it would be mine. After what seemed like a very long month, I went back to claim the money. I felt I had done the right thing and therefore I could enjoy spending it.

In those days, too, the world of children was sharply divided from the world of adults, and we remained children for much longer than nowadays. The disadvantage was that we often did not express our worries and fears freely as children do nowadays. I remember sitting on the floor trying to read a book. I must have been about five I suppose. I kept meeting the word 'put' which in my head I pronounced as though it rhymed with 'but' and of course it made no sense. It never occurred to me to ask an older person and be told it rhymed with 'foot'!

I also hated walking home from Brownies in the winter in the dark by myself, but never refused to go or demanded that someone should meet me. I just counted the number of lampposts, cheering myself on by thinking, 'I've gone a quarter of the way', 'Now I'm half-way', 'Only a quarter left', 'Almost there', 'Home!'

~ *Chapter 2* ~

Schooldays

My life as a child, in the early nineteen-thirties, revolved round my family, my school, my Sunday School and my friends. It was at the private school and also at Sunday School that I met my friend Joyce Bland, later Mrs Joyce Dudding. We both had piano lessons too with Miss Annie E. Irwin Dodd, which was another common interest. I often went to Joyce's house, where there was more space, as she was an only child. I sometimes stayed the night and this was in the days before 'sleepovers' were common with children. We were always painting and making things to sell at the 'bazaars' frequently held at our church to raise money. Remarkably there were two pianos in their sitting room, one of them a 'grand'. We played our duets on the upright one.

Myself and Joyce, 50 years later in Derbyshire

It seemed as though we were always moving. My father, at the height of his prosperity, made his final move in Winchmore Hill from Green Dragon Lane to a newly-built house in Downes Court (near the very posh Broad Walk). We decided to call it 'Dunsekin' ('Done Seeking') because we were all convinced that we would now settle down and stop moving. Little did we know!

Joyce and I then added a new activity - going to play in the nearby Grovelands Park. Here there was a large lake and also a lovely little wood with squirrels scampering about, and a little stream running through it. We invented a game called 'jumping the stream', which kept us occupied for hours. There were various 'jumps' all the way along the stream - some easy and some difficult

- we delighted in this simple sport. Nobody worried about us in those days as long as we returned home promptly for meals. We also went to swim at Barrowell Road swimming pool, sometimes before breakfast! I can't remember learning to swim - we certainly never had lessons that we paid for. We just struggled - swallowing gallons of water in the process - picking it up somehow, like learning to ride a bicycle. As we grew older we went roller-skating, then progressed to ice-skating, and went further and further afield on our bicycles.

Grovelands Park

Every summer my father rented a house in Worthing near the sea. My mother, Lily, Doreen, Jean, Peter and I went there for a whole month and what a wonderful month it was! We really ran wild and enjoyed ourselves playing on the beach, swimming in the sea, building sandcastles and occasionally going to the pier to play on the slot machines and perhaps go in a boat. I suppose there were days when it was wet and chilly, but I don't remember them. I only remember the gorgeously hot ones. Of course it wasn't much of a holiday for Mum and Lily as there were still meals to be prepared and housework to be done and I don't think the children gave much help. Dad came down at weekends. When it was time to go home we were all as brown as berries, having soaked up sun and fresh sea air, ready to face the winter, which was longer and more severe in those days.

Once home we fell back into our usual routine of school and weekends. Almost every Saturday we went to spend our pocket money at Woolworths in Palmers Green, saving some of it to go to the cinema. There were three to choose from - the Capital in Winchmore Hill (now an office block), the Queens (very old and run-down) and the Palladium in Palmers Green. How I loved Spencer Tracy in 'Captains Courageous'; and how I wept over John Clement's predicament in 'The Four Feathers' - but I think that was later on after 1937.

I was in my early teens when we moved to Downes Court, and when we went for our usual summer holiday at Worthing, I remember sitting on the beach with my mother who had obviously planned for us to be alone. She carefully explained what I should expect when I started menstruating. She was nervous and had obviously rehearsed her speech. I was embarrassed and pleased when the 'talk' was over.

Schooldays

When I finally discovered from a friend in my class how babies were conceived, I remember being outraged. Not about the sexual act itself, which I found highly intriguing and interesting. But to think that grown-ups at school and at home had taught me so many things, but had allowed me to reach the age of thirteen without telling me this highly important fact! I felt I could never trust adults again!

On Sunday in those days many children went to Sunday School even if their parents (like mine) didn't go to church. It was held on Sunday afternoons from 3 - 4 and the adults were pleased to have a couple of hours' peace and quiet. Joyce and I went to the Winchmore Hill Methodist Church Sunday School. It was run very efficiently by one Mr Lowther and his team of dedicated young men and women including my sister Lily. Apparently Mr Lowther (who was also very musical) had had to choose between being the Sunday School Superintendent (an important post in the church in those days) and choirmaster (a post with even more status).

Every year we had the Sunday School Anniversary, which was a grand occasion. The children's choir - of course trained by Mr Lowther himself - practiced for weeks beforehand and occupied the choir stalls for the two services on THE DAY. A special speaker was invited and we all felt tremendously important. I can still remember how we all sang with great feeling:

> It is a thing most wonderful,
> Almost too wonderful to be,
> That God's own son should come from heaven,
> And die to save a child like me!

Although we hardly knew the word 'theology' we readily embraced the mystery of the Christian life. We instinctively knew that we were insignificant compared with the power, majesty and holiness of the God we worshipped, and yet we were amazingly important in God's sight because he loved us and His Son died for us. We were cut down to size and yet at the same time we could hold our heads high. Somehow we grasped the paradox. Maybe this gave our generation stability and generally made us happier and easier to control in the home and the classroom. We had not yet begun to ask why it was necessary for Jesus to die for us, in order to save us, or what he was saving us from.

The Sunday school was not only lively but also very much mission-orientated. There was an organisation called the J.M.A. (Juvenile Missionary Association), which is still running I believe. We scampered around collecting money every week from our subscribers, trying to outdo our friends to see who could collect the most! As we had many speakers from abroad we were quite well educated about other countries.

We took it for granted that these countries had flourishing churches full of well-educated people, much like our own church.

Schooldays

We didn't grow up with the idea that countries in the Third World were full of starving and 'primitive' people waiting for our help, even though we collected money for them. Another paradox! Among the congregation was a retired minister, Rev Harold Rattenbury who had once been a missionary in China. He later became the President of the Methodist conference. Through his wife Emily's influence I became fired with the ambition to become a missionary myself - of course in China! Little did I know that God had other more interesting plans for me!

At Sunday School I remember hearing the story of 'Aggrey of Africa' - Dr James Emman Kwegyir Aggrey born at Anomabu in the Gold Coast. A man of fine intellect, he refused to let racial prejudice sour his fine and generous character. When he travelled on a ship to America, it was not considered fitting for a black man to sit at a table for meals with the white passengers, so he had his own small table and ate alone. He made a joke of it, saying that he was lucky to receive special and fast service because his waiter only had one person to serve. I was greatly impressed by many of his philosophical sayings, such as 'If you educate a man, you only educate an individual, but if you educate a woman, you educate a family.' Using the piano as an illustration, he also said, 'You can play a tune of sorts on the black keys only, and you can play a tune of sorts on the white keys only, but for perfect harmony you must use both the black and the white keys.' I was inspired by his story at a time when I had no idea that I would one day live in the Gold

Coast and be married to a Gold Coaster.

While we were at Downes Court, my half-brother, Ken, married Ella Robertson, and that was a very happy occasion. Ken had by this time, followed in our father's footsteps and become a butcher. He and Ella lived in the house in Green Dragon Lane and Aunt Mary moved to a flat in Fernleigh Road.

Not so long after this, my father had pneumonia very badly. Of course there were no antibiotics in those days and everything depended on good nursing. Like many people of his generation, my father had a horror of going to hospital, so nurses were employed to care for him at home. My young brother Peter and myself were sent to live with Ken and Ella until the crisis was over. Apart from being worried about my father, we enjoyed the experience, and Ken coped admirably with running the shops. One happy result of my father's illness was that he finally (and rather reluctantly) agreed to buy a car. It was Lily who learnt to drive it, and this gave her life a tremendous boost.

As a result of his illness, too, my father decided to retire early - he was in his late fifties - and so we moved yet again, this time to Worthing in Sussex. Once again I stayed with Ken and Ella to finish the academic year at Winchmore Hill High School, and by this time they had a baby, Richard. He was one of twins, the other one being a boy who died at birth or was still-born. Later, Ella became pregnant again but was very ill with high blood pressure. Although she was made to stay in bed for several months, she eventually lost the baby – this time a girl. This was a great source of sorrow to Ella especially as she was advised not to become pregnant again. So she and Ken adopted a baby girl, Susan, who brought them much joy.

When I joined the family in Worthing I was suddenly flung into the big state secondary school there. Of course the private school in Winchmore Hill, although a very happy place and capable of giving us a good education at the primary level, did not have the laboratories and other facilities for science, music and art that the Worthing High School for Girls had. I suddenly found I was very much behind in some subjects.

Jean

My two sisters had left school by this time, and Doreen was working as a hairdresser. Jean had never been very happy at school and, looking back, it was quite possible that she was dyslexic or had some other problem which was not recognised at that time. However she loved animals, and our move to Worthing enabled her to work at a nearby riding stables where she looked after and exercised horses. She loved her new and satisfying life. But of course the problem was that Lily was allergic to all animals and the slightest contact with them brought on attacks of asthma. Even though Jean changed into and out of her working clothes in the garage, it was still a problem.

Perhaps this was why Lily decided to 'leave home' in Worthing and return to London. She didn't want to prevent Jean from pursuing her chosen career. She also missed the Winchmore Hill Methodist Church and all her friends there, especially Mabel Watts, a geography teacher, who much later married Rev Reginald Frayn, a retired Methodist minister. Lily went to live with Aunt Mary in her flat in Fernleigh Road although they had little in common and hardly did anything together. They both worked in the butcher shops as cashiers during the week and went their own way at weekends. At first Lily found it very difficult and different from the life she had lived in a large family for almost twenty years. Feeling homesick, she was often tempted to rejoin the family, but determined to make a complete break she gradually settled down to her new life.

Schooldays

We didn't stay in Worthing for long as my father was never really happy being retired, and as soon as World War II started and the butchers' shops were short of manpower, he made this the excuse to go back to Winchmore Hill and help. My mother also wanted to get away from the coast because with her rather vivid imagination she could see the invading German soldiers running up the beaches and killing everyone in sight! We were more upset that we had to give up our beach hut, and hated to see the beach, where we had spent many happy hours, covered with barbed wire.

So back we went to London, which was going to be even more dangerous once the bombing started. Dad rented a house in Orpington Road (keeping the house in Worthing as well). By this time my old school had closed, and so I went to another state school just in time to do my O-levels as the GCSE was called in those days. Previously I had been to single-sex schools. Now at the age of fifteen or sixteen it was quite exciting to go to a mixed school where there were boys as well as male teachers.

Here I met up with a friend from Sunday School days, Doreen Sear (later Mrs Doreen Page) who also lived in Orpington Road. We used to walk to school together and were joined on the way by Betty Thackeray (later Mrs Betty Saunders). There was always a good deal of chattering and laughing especially on the way home! Doreen was a year ahead of me. I managed to catch up by doing my A-levels in one year instead of two. If I hadn't done this I would have been called up into the Forces but if one had a place at university one was exempt. I didn't do terribly well but at least I didn't have a nervous breakdown as someone predicted I would.

By this time my old friend Joyce Bland had been sent to a Methodist boarding school in Cornwall to be away from the dangers of London, but of course we met up in the holidays. I remember her father taking us up into their attic one fateful evening in 1940 when the whole of the centre of London was ablaze. The scene was frightening. Our school lessons, too, were constantly being interrupted when as soon as the 'Air Raid Warning' sounded we all marched to the tunnel-like air raid shelters in the playground where we sat in darkness, very squashed and very bored, until the 'All Clear' sounded.

My father found life very stressful. It probably worried him that he couldn't give his customers the good quality meat that they were used to, and he probably wasn't making as much money as he would have liked.

Because the German air force (the Luftwaffe) were dropping bombs in built-up areas in large cities like London, people were building Anderson shelters in their gardens. These were strong one-room structures (supplied by the government), half-buried in the ground, with earth heaped on top to protect the people inside from bomb blasts. They were quite small measuring less than two metres by one and a half metres, and cost only £7. We were worried that while our friends' fathers were busily getting these garden shelters built, our father seemed to be doing nothing.

Schooldays

When an air-raid warning sounded, our friends would go into their Anderson shelters with warm clothes, blankets, some food and hot drinks in flasks, as well as lamps or torches for some lighting. There they would stay, sometimes all night, until the 'All Clear' sounded. Meanwhile we were crouching in the cupboard under the staircase, which was supposed to be the safest place if a house was hit. At last we got a Morrison shelter inside the house. This was like a very strong table , made of steel, and we all slept under it.

Although things were not going well, with the retreat from Dunkirk in France, and the air raids, we all were convinced that the country was right to go to war. With God on our side, we were confident that we would win in the end. When several young men we knew and admired who had declared themselves pacifists earlier on, suddenly appeared at church in army or air force uniform we did not blame them for changing their views. Churchill's speeches fired us with determination to defeat the wicked dictators Hitler and Mussolini - although of course we knew nothing about concentration camps like Belsen and Auschwitz, where thousands of people were systematically being put to death simply because they were Jews.

Although life was difficult and bombs were dropping, the church was still a lively place. Mrs Rattenbury, in spite of her rather severe and plain looks, got on well with the teenagers and organized a weekly Bible Fellowship at her house. Later she organized several residential Missionary 'Conferences' for young people at Bishops Stortford. This was an amazing experience for us to be among so many people young and old with a strong Christian faith. Some of the speakers had served abroad and had interesting stories to tell. It was inspiring and it was fun. Apart from the appeal to heart and soul, the Christian faith made sense intellectually.

Missionary Conference - Mrs Rattenbury third from left

After one of these conferences I remember going home on cloud nine really hoping to convert the whole family to my way of thinking. Apart from Lily (no longer living with us), I was the only member of the family who was a member of the church and who went regularly. The moment passed, I came down to earth and we all continued as before! My mother with great perception realized what had happened and gave me quiet support in my disappointment. In return I gave her support when she was absolutely terrified in the air raids as we crouched together under the stairs.

~ Chapter 3 ~

Meeting Michael at University

I now realized, in the early nineteen-forties, when the war was raging, that there was the possibility that I could go to university. Doreen Sear and I both applied to Queen Mary College, University of London, and were accepted. Because of the war the college was evacuated to the University of Cambridge and we were based at King's College. There was a hostel for the female students but we did not get places there and were 'billeted' with Mr and Mrs Rider in Holbrook Road. Again because of the war, civilians were obliged to give accommodation to the armed forces, or government workers or evacuees if it was needed. I think the Riders thought it was in their best interest to take a couple of supposedly harmless female students rather than wait to have soldiers or evacuees thrust upon them. They looked after us very well and we were very happy there. The Riders had no children but their household included Ivy the maid and Martin the cat! Doreen had never ridden a bicycle as a child and so had to learn this important skill before we went to Cambridge where the students cycled everywhere.

Before we went off, there were two weddings in my family. First of all my eldest sister, Doreen, married Jim Morrison on 24th August 1940 at the Winchmore Hill Methodist Church where Lily and I were members. Then in 1941 my other sister Jean married Jack Praill whom she had met in Worthing. I must say I do not remember the occasions all that clearly. Their lives seemed far removed from mine and they seemed much older than I was. Both their husbands were in the forces and both of them had their first child a year or so after they married. They were, therefore, wives of men fighting for their country and mothers of young children while I was still a student hoping to go to university and poring over my books. In fact I was to get married about ten years later even though I was only three or four years younger than they were.

It was in 1942 that Doreen Sear and I went to Cambridge and we considered that we were very lucky to be there. Although not technically Cambridge University students, we enjoyed all the activities going on there. We immediately joined MethSoc, the society for Methodist students, and every Sunday afternoon went to the Manse for tea and hymn singing, and went to a weekly

Meeting Michael at University

fellowship group where we made friends. In the holidays too we joined in various activities. On one occasion we went hiking in the Lake District, staying at Youth Hostels and managed to scale Scafell Pike. On another occasion we went to St Andrews in Scotland for a Student Christian Movement conference.

Scafell Pike - myself second from right with Doreen

On both occasions Doreen and I 'hitchhiked' there - that is to say, we stood by the side of the road with our rucksacks over our shoulders and got lifts from drivers going our way, mostly lorry drivers. Outside all the railway stations at that time there were large notices reading 'Is your journey REALLY necessary?' so we considered we were being very patriotic to travel in this way. I wonder that our parents - especially our mothers - allowed us to do this, because nowadays it would be considered extremely

51

Myself

dangerous. But we didn't have any unpleasant experiences.

I was reading English and Doreen was reading German. I was very much out of my depth partly because I had rushed through the A-level (or rather the Intermediate as it was called then) in one year and partly because of my family background. We were not in the habit of having intellectual conversations at home! I was the first member of my family to dream of going to university. In fact in those days there were relatively few girls who did. I also did not realize that reading English involved studying Old English and Middle English texts. They were like foreign languages to me: I probably should have chosen another subject!

Meeting Michael at University

It was in my second year that I met Michael. He was older than I was but in those days it took the Gold Coast students longer to complete their schooling. It was about three weeks after the beginning of the first term of our second year, and Doreen and I went to the Manse as usual on Sunday afternoon. The Rev Spivey was the chaplain for the students. I saw this young African looking rather lost - and without the necessary hymn book. It turned out that the convoy of ships he was travelling with was delayed and indeed they nearly got torpedoed on the way. Therefore he and his friends were late arriving for the academic year. I offered my hymn book to Michael and shared with Doreen, and that was the beginning of our friendship.

I remember the first time I was invited to his room at Queens' College for tea. We became friends and went out together from time to time. He was always one to take his studies very seriously and didn't want too many distractions. Although I didn't realize it at the time, he had been sent to Cambridge privately by his father, who had had quite a high position in the Post Office but was now retired. He was not on a government scholarship as were many of his friends. He could not afford to waste time or fail any exams. After completing the Cambridge Natural Sciences tripos he then got a scholarship to do medicine at St Bartholomew's Hospital (Barts), London.

On February 29th 1944 my father died. He had been ill for some time but it was still a great shock to me. He never met

Michael, of whom I'm sure he would have initially disapproved because he was quite prejudiced against 'foreigners' (including those who were white!). I like to think that he would have been won round by his character and his charm. My mother certainly was.

Dad

I held our Head of Department, Professor James Sutherland, in the highest regard, but didn't get on too well with the female lecturers who were very academic and sometimes very sarcastic. I liked Prof Sutherland even more when he wrote my testimonial at the end of my course (this was much later), and praised me for carrying on bravely after the death of my father. I only managed

Meeting Michael at University

to get a lower second degree but he also mentioned that one of my papers was first class. This really encouraged me in the years ahead. I also learnt a valuable lesson as a teacher that a little praise works wonders!

After two years, and before we finished our degree course, Doreen and I were required to do some national service or train to be a teacher. She went to Bletchley Park, which at that time was the home of the Government Communications Headquarters (GCHQ) now well-known and functioning at Cheltenham. There at Bletchley Park they were successfully cracking the German secret codes. Naturally they were not allowed to talk about their highly confidential work and I don't think I realized how closely Doreen was involved in helping to win the war.

I went to the Institute of Education, which was part of the University of London. I sometimes wish I had joined the Forces just for the experience of being part of the war effort. The uniforms of the women's ATS (Auxiliary Territorial Service), WAAF (Women's Auxiliary Air Force) and WRNS (Women's Royal Naval Reserve - usually referred to as 'Wrens') sections of the army, air force and navy were very attractive too. However I knew I wanted to teach and I still vaguely wanted to go abroad as a missionary. Once again those who went into teaching were exempt from being called up. By the time I finished the one-year teacher's Diploma Course the war had ended and we were then allowed to return to Queen Mary College and complete our degree course. It was now back at Mile End Road in the East End of London, which had been badly bombed. Luckily the college itself was still standing and was quickly made usable. It was while I was doing my teacher's training that the medical exam revealed that I had a hearing problem. It was not very severe, and the doctor said he would pass me. He added that he knew I would get married, and in those days, most married women became full-time housewives, and would expect their husbands to be the breadwinners. How old-fashioned that sounds now!

Soon after my father died, my mother went back to Worthing. Peter was called up and served in Egypt but fortunately was not in any active fighting. My sister Doreen went off with Jim to Catterick and later Anglesey. Jack was in the forces that fought their way along the North African coast and through Italy. While Jack was abroad, Jean lived in the flat over the No 1 shop (as it was called) on the Broadway, Winchmore Hill, and worked in the shop below. As I was now studying back in London I often lived there with her. From the flat window I enjoyed watching the people bustling about shopping, and then the sudden change of mood at closing time. I celebrated my twenty-first birthday there. Because of our recent bereavement and the fact that we were all scattered, nobody seemed to notice the fact and I was quite upset. Ken saved the day by taking me to the theatre to see a musical. Doreen Sear spent the weekend with me, and gave me a Methodist hymn book, with tunes, on India paper and with a zip

Meeting Michael at University

to close it - I have the book to this day!

A week later, on May 8th 1945, we celebrated the end of the war in Europe. It was called 'VE (Victory in Europe) Day', and there was great rejoicing because it had been almost six long weary years of struggle with plenty of loss of life. Fighting was still going on in the Far East against Japan. Three months later Doreen was again staying with me at the flat - I suppose Jean had gone off, probably to meet Jack who was on leave. It was August Bank Holiday Monday, 1945, and we turned on the radio only to hear the shattering news of the dropping of the atomic bomb on Hiroshima. We were stunned and shocked, and somehow ashamed that our own country was involved in this horrific slaughter of innocent human beings. Of course we were told that it would shorten the war and save many lives, but that didn't seem to make it any better. We felt life - and war - would never be the same again. The celebration of the end of the war against Japan - 'VJ (Victory against Japan) Day' came soon afterwards.

Now that the war was over we were free to go back to Queen Mary College for our final year and finish our degrees. Jean was reunited with Jack and living in Worthing, so I had to make another move, this time to stay with my mother's sister Auntie Edie and her husband Uncle Fred at Arnos Grove. About this time too my relationship with Michael was becoming a bit more serious. It obviously couldn't stand still. Then I really got cold feet.

At that time there were few mixed marriages and I realized what a big step it would be. Did I really want to get involved with such a complicated situation? What about any children of such a marriage? Would they feel 'different' and not fit in? Such questions may seem ridiculous nowadays with so many mixed marriages around, but in those days were quite real. I told Michael that I did not want to go out with him any more. Maybe that was the reason why I chose to go and teach at boarding schools far from London when I finished my training. I thought the change of scene would help me forget him and perhaps I could move on to a new relationship.

Somehow we got back together again! He was always one to get his own way without appearing to force the issue! That was one of his great strengths when later dealing with difficult colleagues. Anyway I was quite miserable without him and pleased to think once again of our future together in spite of all the difficulties.

Some years were to pass before we could think of getting married. Michael was still in the middle of his medical course and in those days budding doctors did not marry before they qualified and certainly did not live with 'partners' as they might do today. What a frustrating situation!

~ Chapter 4 ~

A Year in Nigeria

The war was over and it was now 1947. The best way forward (in my opinion) was for me to get a job in the Gold Coast so that I could see for myself what life out there was like and whether I could cope. We never considered it a possibility that we would settle in England because Michael was then on a scholarship and 'bonded' to go back. In any case I could see that he desperately wanted to go back and was quite homesick at times.

I offered my services to the Methodist Missionary Society and was accepted, but they could only send me to Nigeria, not the Gold Coast! Michael's friends were horrified! All Gold Coasters thought their country was by far 'the best' and that they were a cut or two above all other Africans, and that I would be thoroughly put off if I went to Nigeria. Michael and I weren't so pessimistic and off I went to teach at the Methodist Girls' High School in Lagos. The usual way of getting there was by mail boat - the Elder Dempster Line - which took ten days, stopping at Las Palmas in the Canary Islands; then either Bathurst (Gambia) or Freetown (Sierra Leone); then Takoradi in the Gold Coast; and finally Lagos in Nigeria. It was a wonderful trip and I enjoyed every minute of it. Most of the passengers were European as this was ten years before independence, and they were nearly all colonial civil servants with a sprinkling of missionaries.

Mail Boat - Apapa

Of course it became hotter and hotter as we went south but we had a swimming pool to keep us cool. All the crew changed into their white tropical uniforms, and, after wartime Britain, everything seemed to be quite luxurious with lavish meals and all

A Year in Nigeria

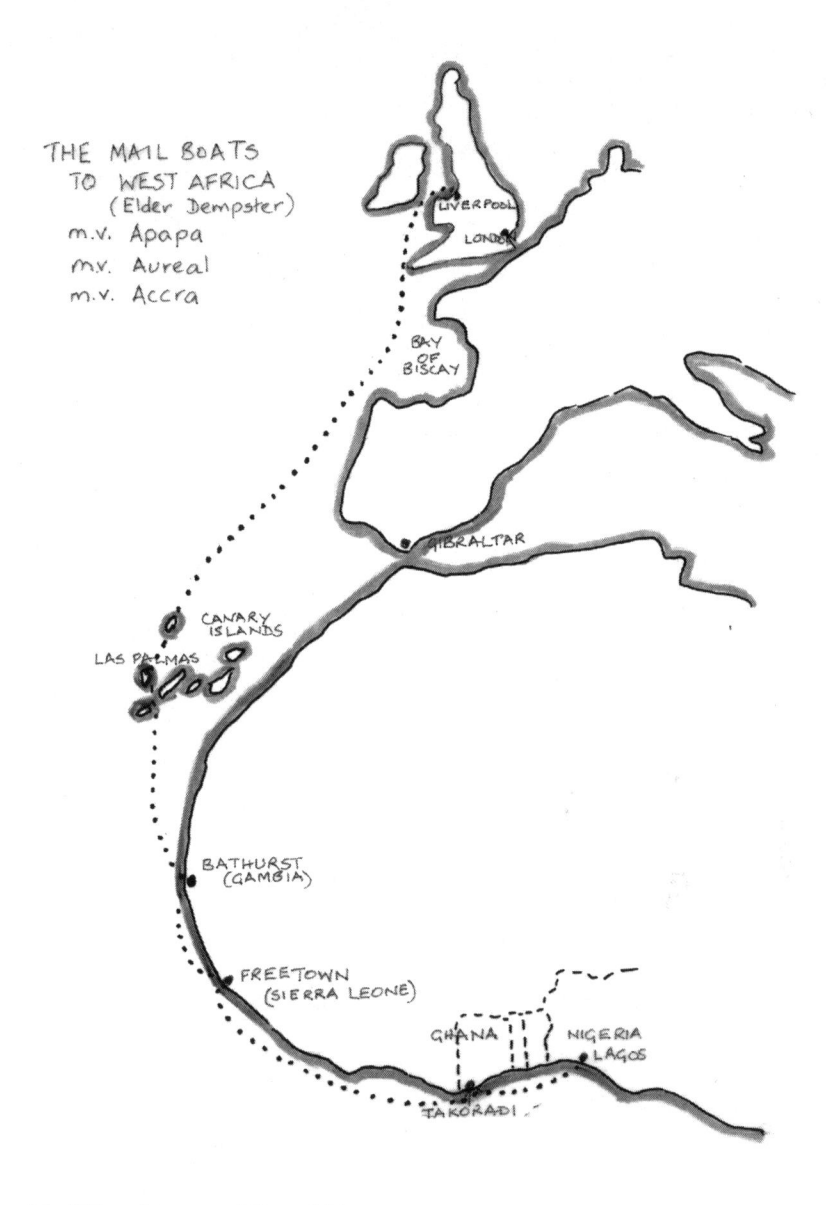

Mail Boat Route to West Africa

sorts of entertainment. I caught my first glimpse of Africa, which I found quite thrilling especially when we docked briefly at Takoradi. I remember on the day after I arrived in Lagos and settled in at the school, I decided to go for a short walk. With my head in the clouds, I walked straight into one of the open drains typical of British urban Africa - up to my shoulders! Fortunately I wasn't hurt but a bit shaken. Fortunately too it was a completely dry and clean drain! I came down to earth and was more careful after that.

Unusually the Methodist Girls' High School was a day school but every Friday afternoon Dorothy Verney (the headmistress), Mildred (another missionary) and myself went visiting the girls in their homes. Most were Christians but a few were Muslims. This was an interesting experience and the girls (and their families) were delighted when it was their turn to be visited.

The usual length of one 'tour' in those days was fifteen months, so I was there for three school holidays. During one of them, I visited many of the missionaries up country and they kindly showed me as much of the local scene as possible. On another occasion I went by air to visit Michael's family, staying with another missionary Rose Little. Michael's family were all very welcoming. Michael's father, then retired, spoke impeccable English. His six sisters (he had no brothers) were educated and also spoke English.

A Year in Nigeria

Michael's father, Peter

His mother, Sybilla, was the most 'traditional', and did not speak much English, and of course I did not speak Ga, but we got on very well. Her maiden name was 'Vanderpuye', and she was descended from Henry Hood Vanderpuye, who was born in 1858 and died in 1942. Henry was one of three brothers of mixed race, originally from Elmina. It is interesting to note that there was a Dutchman called Jacobus Van der Puye, who was governor at Elmina Castle from 10th March, 1780 to 30th December, 1780. I have never been able to discover whether there was any connection between this governor and the three brothers, Peter, Henry and John.

Michael's mother, Sybilla

Back to my own situation, and my visit to my prospective father-, mother- and sisters-in-law! They prepared a huge meal for me which I could hardly do justice to. It was an interesting experience and heart-warming too. I felt I could 'fit in', and Rose Little certainly did not try to put me off the idea of marrying a Gold Coaster.

I returned to Lagos and continued teaching. I enjoyed it up to a point but living in a missionary compound and mixing with respectful Nigerian students and teachers at work, and Europeans in one's spare time, didn't really give any indication of what it would be like married to an African and living in Africa permanently, bringing up a family. Looking back I wonder that I didn't become more friendly with some of the Nigerian teachers of my own age. Somehow they didn't expect it and I wasn't encouraged to do so. Although the missionaries were doing good work it was very much a case of 'them' and 'us'.

However I certainly realized how difficult the West African climate was - extremely humid and the temperature, though not extremely high, was always about 28 to 30 degrees centigrade. No cool nights to look forward to and no cool seasons. The days were almost the same length all the year round - no long light summer evenings. It seemed very monotonous: the only difference was between the wet and the dry seasons. I longed for my tour of fifteen months to be over, so that I could go on furlough (as it was called).

As the time drew near, I thought how nice it would be to visit Michael's family once more on my way home. The mail boats only stopped at Takoradi and it would be impossible to get to Accra (240 kilometres away) and back in the time available. The only alternative was to get on a cargo boat which was stopping at Accra. These were few and far between and rather irregular but at last I succeeded. The ship was stopping at Accra to load cocoa and would be there for ten days. Unfortunately after we had been at sea for 24 hours the captain announced that he had received a cable instructing him to stop at Lome in Togo instead and load cocoa there. I was furious because I had waited so long for this ship, and the captain said he would be anchored off Lome for three weeks!

The Captain also got annoyed and said that if I wanted to I could get off his ship, make my own way to Accra and rejoin the ship at Takoradi in three weeks' time. To his surprise I did so. I got off with some hand luggage, wandered round Lome, saw a sign indicating that some missionaries lived in a certain building, went inside and told them my problem.

They were very sympathetic and said they knew a Gold Coaster, one Mr Baeta, who worked for the UAC., a big foreign commercial firm, at Keta in the Gold Coast. However his wife and children lived in Lome in Togo so he visited them frequently. The distance was quite short. As you know, the border between the Gold Coast and Togoland runs right through the land occupied by the Ewes, so families were often separated in this way.

They arranged with him to give me a lift to Keta where I slept overnight at the Rest House, and then he put me on the ferry across the lagoon. I got off on the other side and got a lift in a lorry that was going to Accra (more hitchhiking!). There I made my way to Miss Rose Little, later visited the Baddoos and then got a lift to Methodist missionaries in Cape Coast. I was made welcome and thoroughly enjoyed my stay. Every day they would phone Takoradi to see when my ship was due in. However when they heard that I hadn't had my passport stamped when crossing the border with Mr Baeta they thought I might have a problem.

Because Mr Baeta crossed the border so many times to visit his family, the officials just waved us through.

I really don't know whether the missionaries at Cape Coast were genuinely worried or whether they were teasing me a little! At that time in the late forties the atmosphere was rather tense in the Gold Coast. The people were demanding 'Independence NOW!' and there was the famous incident of three people being shot at the crossroads at Christiansburg in Accra. This happened in 1948 when a British police officer gave the command to open fire on a crowd of unarmed demonstrators, and three ex-servicemen died. After this, the attitude towards the colonial rulers became soured and people were even more determined to gain independence. Officially I wasn't in the country at all so how could I get out?

I must say I became nervous myself but managed to get out of the dilemma. There were only six or eight of us (all Europeans) boarding this ship, which was anchored off shore. We were going in a small motor launch and at the quayside a few officials were there to stamp our passports at a little table. When a few people had been dealt with and had moved to one side I managed to edge my way round and joined them without going to the table. I rather admired my own resourcefulness! And you should have seen the Captain's face when he saw me coming up the ladder! I don't think he expected I would succeed in making my way from Lome to Takoradi. In fact he was astonished to see me again.

To Ghana with Love

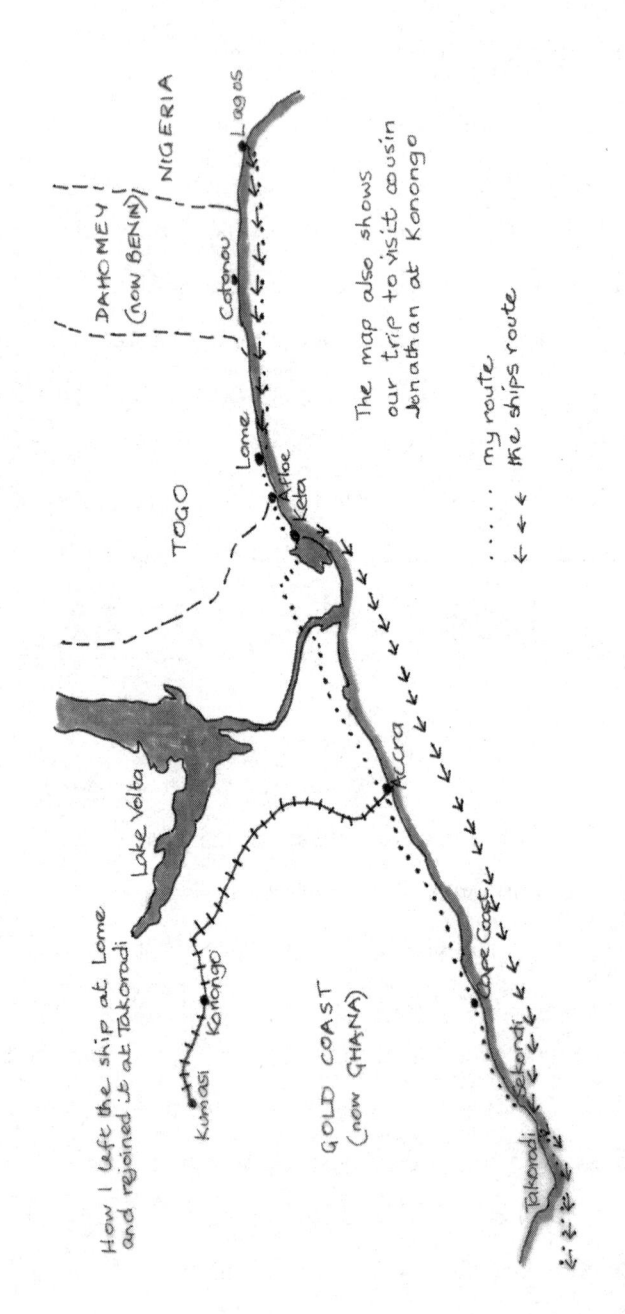

Route from Lagos to Takoradi

A Year in Nigeria

I didn't really enjoy the trip home as the Captain and passengers were not my type at all. The Captain was a bit of a racist, and the burly middle-aged policewoman I shared my cabin with was a real 'colonialist'. I could well imagine her throwing her weight about and lording it over 'the natives'. Michael was waiting for me when we docked in London. We gave each other a warm embrace, and I wasn't sure whether I hoped they were all too busy disembarking to notice, or whether I wanted them to see us and have another surprise. I had certainly never mentioned Michael or our future plans on the ship.

~ *Chapter 5* ~

Marriage and Motherhood

Soon after I got back, Michael qualified as a doctor and we felt we could at last get married. It was just about this time, too, that the papers were full of the story of an English girl, Ruth Williams who married Seretse Khama in 1948. He was the traditional ruler of Bechuanaland (now Botswana), a neighbouring country of South Africa, where at that time, under apartheid, marriages between blacks and whites were illegal - how ridiculous that sounds now! He was studying law at Oxford. The British government and the Anglican Church thought the marriage inadvisable and did everything possible to block it. However Ruth and Seretse were determined and got married at the Kensington Registry office. Even then the British government blocked their return to Bechuanaland (then under

British rule) as the South African president Dr Malan threatened to withhold uranium and gold if this mixed-marriage couple set foot in Africa. The whole affair became a cause célèbre.

Many years later their story was told by Michael Dutfield in a fascinating book called 'A Marriage of Inconvenience'. This book is now unfortunately out of print. Of course my marriage to Michael was completely mundane by comparison but I found Ruth and Seretse's story enthralling, even though I did not know then how successful their marriage was going to be and how Ruth would die in Botswana at the age of 78, greatly loved and respected by the people. Then, I simply admired her courage and although our situations were so very different I took her as my role model.

It is strange that more than fifty years later I am enjoying reading the cult series of books, set in Botswana, 'The No 1 Ladies Detective Agency' by Alexander McCall Smith. These books, more than any UN resolutions, help to correct the common negative view of Africa as a place of insoluble problems. Instead, chapter after chapter, we follow some wonderful people full of the desire and ability to solve problems, as well as having faults and failings just like everyone else.

Botswana (a country not without its problems especially with regard to HIV/AIDS) is one of the least corrupt in Africa, and has remained peaceful using the wealth from its diamonds wisely. Seretse's rule with his wife Ruth by his side must have had something to do with that. She never interfered in political affairs but was active in charitable organisations.

To go back to my own situation, Michael and I had a quiet wedding on May 20th 1950 at the Winchmore Hill Methodist Church, which had had such an influence on my life. This was about seven years after we first met - we certainly hadn't rushed into it! As my father had died, I asked Ken if he would 'give me away'. He confessed that he did not want to do this and I was taken aback. I can remember the moment clearly in my mother's sitting room! She had sold the house in Worthing and moved back to North London and was living at 46 Green Moor Link. After a stunned silence, it flashed into my mind that he would probably be greatly teased by the other shopkeepers on the Broadway for giving away his sister to a 'black' man and I actually felt sorry for him and said, 'Oh, don't worry, it's all right! Now, how about a cup of tea?'

At that time – and even today – many people disapproved of mixed marriages especially between blacks and whites. But there are practical reasons for welcoming them. We all know that in some communities there is a lot of intermarriage between close relatives and this often leads to some serious health problems such as a high incidence of deafness. Of course, mixed marriages often do the opposite, and have a beneficial effect, reducing the incidence of difficult diseases like sickle-cell anaemia.

In England, we are already a very mixed lot because the Angles, Saxons, Vikings, French and many persecuted people from other countries have come and settled here. Some people think this is what has made Great Britain great! Now we have Pakistanis, Indians, people from numerous African countries, Chinese and many others coming in, and this time they are not white. But why should that be a problem? We should also remember too, that mixed marriages will always be in the minority, as people tend to marry people from the same background as themselves.

Later I asked Uncle Fred, married to my aunt Edie, if he would give me away and he was delighted to be honoured in this way. We weren't going to have a grand wedding with long gowns and lots of bridesmaids, but I wanted Doreen to be my one bridesmaid. We had become close friends in the two years at Cambridge going through thick and thin together. We had kept in touch when I was in Lagos and she was working in Berlin as an interpreter with the Control Commission. Looking back now over more than sixty years, she has stood by the whole family and given us all tremendous help and support.

Joe (later Dr) Glover was the best man and Rev Pickard conducted the ceremony while Mr Wilkinson played the organ. Doreen and I wore nice outfits with hats and bouquets. My relatives and a few of Michael's Gold Coast friends were invited. Afterwards we went back to my mother's house and she had organized refreshments. Michael changed into his 'kente' cloth

Marriage and Motherhood

Our wedding day

(beautifully hand-woven in long strips which are then sewn together) and I put on a Gold Coast outfit and we took a few photos in the garden. There was a nice relaxed atmosphere. I do remember thinking I would try to have as many children as possible so that if they felt 'different' they could all feel different together. I need not have worried. As so many Gold Coast men were sent to England to study (and very few Gold Coast women) there were plenty of mixed marriages and plenty of mixed-race children.

No honeymoon for us but we simply went to Michael's 'digs' at 42, Hornsey Lane Gardens. The sister of the landlady there had also married Michael's great friend Samuel Azu Crabbe, who was later to become Ghana's Chief Justice. Although Michael had qualified as a doctor with the Conjoint Board, he wanted to take the Cambridge medical qualification too. He went off to Cambridge full of confidence because the night before he had dreamt that he had killed a dangerous snake and, according to him, this always predicted success! He was right. He then started applying for jobs and secured a houseman's job in the Casualty department of the Bradford Royal Infirmary.

I quickly became pregnant and suffered badly from morning sickness, which to me was 'morning-till-night' sickness! I really felt dreadful and this was to happen with every pregnancy. So Michael went off to Bradford and I stayed with Mum for a while. When I felt a little better I joined Michael in Bradford. He had accommodation in the hospital, of course, but I managed to find a couple of rooms in town. I got a job as a cashier in Brown Muffs, a big departmental store. All the cashiers were in one big room and the containers, with cash and receipt, came whizzing to us along overhead wires from all corners of the store. We took the cash, put the change in the container if necessary, stamped the receipt and sent the container whizzing back to the correct counter. I quite enjoyed the experience of doing a job that didn't

Marriage and Motherhood

involve preparing lessons and marking books in one's 'free' time.

A month before I was due, I went back to stay with Mum, and Rosemary was born at the local hospital. Doreen described her saying, 'She's just like Michael but pretty!' There's something very special about one's first child and she really was a sweet little thing. She didn't sleep very well at night and again this seemed to be the rule with all my children. Maybe I wasn't a very skilful mother. Michael was delighted with his first-born and seemed to be able to soothe her to sleep better than I could. But he was not around much.

Uncle Fred, myself, Mum, Rosemary, Michael and Auntie Edie

After Bradford he got another houseman's job at Hove Hospital in Sussex. He did really well in both Bradford and Hove and enjoyed the work immensely. As he proved himself in both places he was given more responsibility and everyone was sorry to see him go. After that he was asked by the Colonial Office to do the Diploma in Tropical Medicine before going back to the Gold Coast. The course was in London so we lived with Mum until he completed it.

It was at this time that my sister Jean was diagnosed with Hodgkin's disease, a type of cancer. The doctors told her husband Jack that she probably only had two years to live. This was a great shock to us all, especially as she had two young children, but Jean herself was not told of the prognosis. I felt I had to visit her with baby Rosemary. She was having treatment, and carrying on cheerfully and was delighted to see us. As well as her love of animals, she had a great fondness for babies and children, and had a remarkable rapport with them. At the end of our visit when she saw me off at the railway station, waving her scarf, and running along the platform as the train left, I really thought I would never see her again. With her positive attitude however, she proved the doctors wrong and lived on for more than ten years instead of two.

When Rosemary was about eighteen months old, we were finally ready to accompany Michael who was returning to his own country, the Gold Coast, after having been away for nearly ten years. Again it was on one of the Elder Dempster ships. Another luxury cruise with all expenses paid! This time there were more

Marriage and Motherhood

West Africans aboard. The British government were looking ahead and training as many as possible to take the place of the British when the West African colonies became independent. Everybody accepted that this would happen and pretty soon.

We were met at Takoradi by some of Michael's relatives and whisked off to Accra. We went straight to the family house at Derby Avenue near James Town where a great crowd of relatives was assembled. At the entrance there was an old man (dressed in traditional 'cloth' of course) holding a sheep. As soon as we arrived he took out a sharp knife and expertly cut the poor creature's throat! I was horrified. Nothing in Nigeria had prepared me for this! I expected to see Rosemary howling with fright but she was looking on quite unconcerned!

After being thoroughly welcomed we went off to stay at the Avenida Hotel. Michael's mother was greatly disappointed that we weren't staying at Derby Avenue. However, at the hotel we were bitten mercilessly by mosquitoes and after a few days did go and stay at the family house. While we were waiting to hear about Michael's posting, and before we got a car, we decided to go by train to visit Michael's cousin, Jonathan Allotey-Pappoe at Konongo (shown on the 'Route from Lagos to Takoradi' map on page 68). We boarded the train at about 8 am and arrived at 5 pm, although the journey was less than 240 kilometres. We stopped at every station, enjoying watching the people and buying fruit and other things the hawkers were selling. It was an interesting trip.

Jonathan met us and even though we were tired, we had to go and greet all his friends in their houses and report our safe arrival. One didn't have visitors in the Gold Coast without sharing them with one's friends. No doubt the fact that I was 'white' added interest.

We then went to Jonathan's home and met his wife Jacoba and his children. Everyone talked non-stop catching up on ten years' news. We had a nice meal and went to bed. We got up early the next morning to catch the train back to Accra. Much to my surprise we had to go and say goodbye to the same people we had greeted the night before. Not to do so would have been a breach of Gold Coast etiquette. I wonder we didn't stay a few days to make it all worthwhile!

At last we heard that Michael had been posted to Effia-Nkwanta Hospital in Sekondi. Michael had bought a car in Accra and, although he hadn't had much experience driving in England, he had passed his driving test there and drove us safely to our new home. I think I am right in saying that there were two other doctors working there at the time - both English and both more senior, one being in charge as Medical Superintendent.

The English matron made us very welcome and had gone to a great deal of trouble getting a bungalow ready for us. It had been a guest house and often unoccupied so it was rather neglected and surrounded by a lot of 'bush'. I suppose this was the reason why we killed six snakes in the first six weeks. On one occasion a snake bit the night watchman, and I (having read a book about what to

Our first car

do in such circumstances!) slashed the bite with a sharp razor to make the blood flow! Michael was out at the time, and when he returned took the man to the hospital. He was treated and recovered with no ill effects. Whether my 'first aid' helped I never knew!

I must say Michael was not as happy working with the two expatriate doctors in his own country as he had been working with English doctors in England. I don't think they were much more experienced or older than he was but they treated him with little respect. I never met them socially. Probably they were unmarried - we were certainly never invited to their bungalows for a meal, but this was understandable if they were bachelors. Things improved slightly when one of them was in difficulties with a forceps delivery, and had to ask Michael to come to the theatre to help him. They solved the problem between them and after that their relationship improved. Part of the trouble was that Michael always looked far younger than his age, and he wasn't one to blow his own trumpet, so people tended to underestimate him!

Another source of irritation concerned 'private practice' which was allowed by the government at that time. Some patients were entitled to free treatment, but others had to pay. Of course the two more senior doctors took all the fee-paying patients, leaving Michael to see those who got free treatment! He thought this was most unfair.

However we saw a lot of an old Gold Coast friend, Mr Boi-Doe, who was a senior Education Officer, and his wife, Elizabeth, and their three children. Elizabeth was very helpful teaching me some Gold Coast cooking and generally showing me the ropes. I must say I was a bit 'lost' and needed a bit of guidance. We also visited Michael's cousin, the Rev Ebenezer Allotey-Pappoe, who was a Methodist minister stationed at Shama. I took some of my worries and problems to his wife, Violet. They had a son, and twin girls Akwele and Akuorkor.

Much later I remember reading that for a mixed marriage to succeed it was advisable, first, for the couple to do their courting in the country where they intended to settle, and second, the country where they settled should be the woman's rather than the man's. The reason for the first rule is that a person does change when he or she is out of his or her own country. I could see that Michael was a different person in the Gold Coast. Not that he was better or worse but just different. Obviously he was no longer homesick and in a sense didn't need me as much as he did in England. Also, as a 'been-to' (someone who had been abroad and studied there), he had much more status in the Gold Coast than in England. I welcomed both these changes for him. I too was probably a different person when away from my own country. Therefore we both had to adapt to a slightly changed partner from the one we had married.

The reason for the second 'rule' was that it was easier for the woman to cope with domestic matters in her own culture and environment. I found shopping and cooking the food Michael obviously preferred quite difficult. I missed being able to push Rosemary around in a pram to keep her quiet and also give myself a bit of exercise. I took a long time getting used to depending on 'seamstresses' instead of buying ready-made clothes. I was no good in the markets where one lost face if one did not do a bit of bargaining, preferably in the local language.

Most of the English girls who married Gold Coasters were in the same situation as myself. We had broken the two golden rules but nevertheless we made a success of our marriages with the help of our very patient and tolerant husbands.

~ *Chapter 6* ~

Life in a New Culture

We gradually settled down at Sekondi in 1952 and the snakes got the message that they were not welcome, going off somewhere else. We even started a vegetable garden and planted some potatoes. Michael knew how much I missed them. Michael's sister Flora (now Mrs Sackeyfio), who was twenty years younger than he was, came to stay, as we were going to be responsible for her education when she went to the secondary boarding school at Cape Coast. Michael's father also came to visit. We were expected to shoulder some family responsibilities especially as Michael's father had paid out a lot of money when Michael first went to Cambridge. In those days, too, people working for the British Colonial Service were quite well off. We didn't mind at all although perhaps it did become a bit of a burden later on. Everything depended on whether Michael was posted to a hospital where he could earn money through 'private practice'.

Flora

While I was in Sekondi I was approached by the Extra-Mural Department of the University College of the Gold Coast (rather like the Workers' Educational Association in England) to give some lectures on Shakespeare, which were well received. I didn't intend working full-time but wanted to use my skills as a teacher in some small way. Of course some of my Gold Coast counterparts who were wives of doctors were seriously pursuing their own careers, even when it meant being separated from their husbands when they were posted to another part of the country. I found this rather strange. But they were more or less expected to do so. In fact they were doing what wives in England do nowadays - fifty years later - working in order to help pay off mortgages and generally contribute to family expenses. It seems as though the Gold Coast wives were ahead of their time.

Of course in the Gold Coast, with so much domestic help available, it was easier for wives to leave their children to go out to work. In January 1953 I did manage to attend the residential annual New Year School run by the Extra-Mural Department. That year it was held at Wesley College, Kumasi. It was at one of the lectures that Peggy Cripps, the daughter of the famous British Chancellor of the Exchequer, Sir Stafford Cripps, put in an appearance. She was questioned closely about the reason for her visit to the Gold Coast, but gave very guarded answers. She and Joe Appiah, the equally famous fighter for independence for the colonies from British rule, had kept their romance a great secret until their wedding in July 1954. He wore 'kente' for the ceremony and the South African press seized on this, printing the picture and calling him a 'Nigerian blanket native'. Joe Appiah was certainly not a Nigerian, and his expensive hand-woven kente cloth was certainly not a blanket!

Much to our surprise, after barely six months in Sekondi, when we were nicely settled, Michael had a telegram telling him to go on transfer to Tamale! We were shocked but had to go, and somehow got the impression that there was no time to be lost. We quickly packed our personal possessions. The bungalows we occupied were always supplied with furniture so that was no problem.

Off we went to Accra where we stayed for a night or two. We left Flora there as she would soon be going to her new school, and took with us a niece Ade (now Mrs Esther Karikari). She was the daughter of Michael's eldest sister Joanna. Then we proceeded to Kumasi where we stayed in the Rest House. The next morning we set off at 5 am as we had been told it was a long journey. Consequently we arrived in Tamale at 1 pm much to everyone's surprise. Not only was it early in the day but also they hadn't expected us for another week at least and there was nowhere for us to stay. First of all we stayed in the 'European' hospital. There was a seriously-ill patient in the ward next door and I had to keep Rosemary as quiet as possible. Quite a task! Then we stayed in the Catering Rest House. By this time we were decidedly short of money. So we mostly lived on bread and sardines. One day we decided to treat ourselves to a meal in the dining room only to find the only thing on the menu was sardine omelettes!

We were finally allocated a bungalow in Residence Road, and one day when Michael was out I received a visit from the wife of the District Commissioner, with vegetables from her garden. In those days all the DC's were European and had considerable status and power as the representative of the British Government.

Life in a New Culture

I felt rather like a newcomer in an English village being welcomed by the lady of the manor.

There was only one other doctor at the Tamale Hospital. He was an expatriate but not an Englishman. Again Michael didn't get on with him. On one occasion they nearly came to blows - this happened not at the hospital but at the Regional Office and a couple of office workers had to hold Michael back or he would have landed a punch! I was completely puzzled. This was so unlike Michael who hardly ever lost his temper or resorted to violence. I couldn't understand it. There must have been some very strong reason for him to react in this way. I can only assume that the expatriate doctor went out of his way to make Michael look small, treating him as he treated the junior nurses, and this Michael could not tolerate especially in front of his fellow Gold Coasters.

The only consolation was that the English Matron did not get on with this expatriate doctor either, and often quietly advised patients to go down to Kumasi for operations as she knew he was attempting cases that he was not competent to deal with. There was no qualified surgeon there at that time but when it was an emergency the theatre nurses preferred to be assisting Michael.

At this time there were only about one hundred government doctors in the country and about half were expatriates and half were Gold Coasters who had all recently qualified. There were a few older Gold Coast doctors in private practice mostly in Accra and Kumasi. Most of the English doctors were good, with a great

Theatre nurses with Michael

deal of experience, and willing to encourage the young Gold Coast doctors who were appearing on the scene in larger numbers year by year. There were just a few expatriates who were not very good and yet thought they could get away with anything in a country like the Gold Coast. They only felt comfortable working with Gold Coasters who were in junior positions. Michael just seemed to have struck unlucky.

Once again we gradually settled down. Tamale was actually a very nice place to be in. There were a lot of Gold Coast civil servants there and they were mostly from the south. At that time the north was greatly behind in development, although they would

Life in a New Culture

My class in Tamale

catch up later on. They had only just established the first secondary school in the north and consequently had produced few graduates. So the Gold Coasters in Tamale were more like expatriates in their own country, feeling a bit lonely and homesick away from their home towns in the south. They all used to gather at the Community Centre where various activities were organized. Again I was roped in by the Tamale branch of the Extra-Mural Department of the University College of the Gold Coast at Legon to give a course of lectures. I was also asked to organize some evening classes for junior civil servants in typing, shorthand and English. There was a Gold Coaster who taught typing and shorthand, while I did the administration and took the English classes.

However the Regional Medical Officer (a very understanding Englishman) was naturally concerned about the poor relationship between the two doctors at the hospital, and thought it best for all concerned that they were separated. I think he also had a high opinion of Michael's competence as a doctor. At first there was the possibility of our going to Bolgatanga in the far north, but finally Michael was posted to Yendi, about 100 kilometres to the east of Tamale. Here he would be the only doctor and would therefore be in charge. He welcomed the idea. I was not so keen as I was again pregnant and again suffering from 'morning-till-night' sickness. We had also had some improvements done to the bungalow in Tamale with the assistance of a very friendly and nice Englishman working for the Public Works Department, and had made ourselves quite comfortable.

Naturally from the moment I arrived in the Gold Coast, I was on a steep learning curve - and made a lot of mistakes! I think most of us who were married to Gold Coasters went through three stages. First of all, one's reaction was that everything was wonderful! (The honeymoon period.) The people were so warm-hearted and welcoming, always smiling and cheerful and ready to help. Then the pendulum swung, and we began to be irritated by the things we were expected to do, or not do. 'What a stupid custom!' 'What a crazy idea!' 'What a dreadful person!' 'Why don't they move with the times?' Finally we reached a happy medium, and realized we were going to meet some wonderful people we would love, and some really nasty characters we would never get on with, just as we would in any country in the world, including our own. We ourselves would change as we went along. At first we would fall over backwards to 'fit in', occasionally making ourselves look ridiculous in the process. Then we might react, and become very awkward, sticking obstinately to our English ways. Finally we would settle for giving way in some situations and being our English selves in others.

It was fortunate in some ways that we were posted away from Michael's home-town, Accra, and were far away first in Sekondi, then in Tamale and Yendi, where my initial mistakes would not be closely scrutinized by my in-laws!

I remember clearly one lesson I learnt in Tamale. We had steward-boys (they were men rather than boys) to help in the house, and one I had employed was really hopeless. I labelled him both lazy and dishonest, because he was always stealing food. I complained bitterly although I was probably the one who had interviewed and employed him as Michael was very busy. After looking at him closely (probably for the first time), Michael sent him down to the hospital for a few tests, and it turned out that he had three serious diseases - hookworm was one, and malaria parasites in his blood another, and also severe anaemia. I vowed never to call anyone 'lazy' again without finding out if they were in good health.

~ Chapter 7 ~

Difficult Days

We had been in the country just over a year, and Yendi was Michael's third posting! Once again, we had no choice but to go! We occupied a bungalow in Yendi that had been built by the Germans, as they previously ruled that part of the Gold Coast. In those days most expatriates were working alone without a wife and certainly without children. It consisted of two small rooms in the centre surrounded by a huge expanse of verandah all the way round. The verandah had wooden louvred shutters, which had to be propped open with long sticks of wood every morning and closed every night. The bungalow also had a thatched roof, which had been infested with bats. The bats had been exterminated but some of their droppings still remained, and fell down when it was windy. Fortunately we had a mosquito net over the bed, which prevented the droppings reaching us when we were sleeping!

Previous occupants had stopped using the two small rooms, in the middle, except to store their belongings, because they were very dark. They had gradually divided up the verandah into bedroom, sitting room, dining room, and pantry. As usual, the kitchen was an outside building with a old-fashioned wood stove. Not only that, but there was no running water and no electricity. Every morning, prisoners came from the local prison and drew water from a well nearby, and filled up all the containers in the kitchen, pantry, and bathroom. To me the prisoners all seemed a harmless friendly lot and I couldn't imagine that any of them had committed any serious crimes. I was very relieved that the well had a closely fitting metal cover over it when it was not in use. Nobody was in danger of falling in.

The drainage was also very basic, using the 'soak-away' system. Pipes took the dirty water outside into a channel in the ground, which led to a soak-away pit. The pit was very deep and full of large stones and had some sort of covering at the top. Every evening too the pressure lamps had to be lit. I was not very good at this and often sat in darkness until Michael returned to do the job.

Michael was the first Gold Coast doctor to be stationed there, and curiously enough the local population took some time to get used to the idea that one of their own people (even though of a

Difficult Days

different ethnic group) was capable of doing this highly specialized job. The first day at work Michael came home at eleven in the morning saying that he had seen all the patients and there was nothing more to do. I was amazed because at Sekondi and Tamale he had been extremely busy. This went on for about a month. The locals were obviously waiting and watching to see if this strange 'black' doctor knew what he was about. After one or two emergencies had been successfully dealt with, the situation changed dramatically and patients came flocking in.

He enjoyed being in charge of his own hospital where he had to cope with everything - medicine, surgery, paediatrics, post-mortems, and public health. While we were there he took the opportunity, as the public health officer, officially to declare the bungalow we lived in unfit for human habitation. Of course it was only after we left that the bungalow was demolished and a more modern one built.

The government had decided to build a lot of Health Centres run by senior nurses and midwives and Michael regularly visited one at Bimbilla nearby. Sometimes I went with him for the ride. Both the Yendi hospital and the Bimbilla Health Centre were working very successfully. Michael always got on well with his more junior staff giving them a lot of respect and encouragement, and at the same time helping them with problems they couldn't deal with.

In Yendi, when I was pregnant and feeling most unwell, Ade (then about twelve) wanted to visit Accra in one of the school holidays. Rosemary (then three), who was very fond of her cousin, wanted to go with her! I felt too ill to argue with a persistent three-year-old. Amazingly, we put them both on the long-distance bus to Kumasi, where they were met by and looked after by Auntie Martha (Mrs Lamptey). Her mother was a cousin of Michael's mother and therefore, by Gold Coast standards, quite a close relative! Then they continued the journey to Accra where they stayed at Derby Avenue for two or three weeks. I worried the whole time they were away, asking myself why I had let a child of twelve take charge of a three-year-old on such a long journey!

When they arrived back, I expected Rosemary to come rushing to give me a big hug. Oh no, she looked at me blankly as much as to say, 'Who on earth are you?' When we got home, she played outside for a couple of hours, occasionally coming to the doorway to peer at me. Finally she came and sat on my lap and clung to me for the next couple of days. Who can understand the mind of a child? I often wonder if it was that trip to Accra into a wholly Ga-speaking environment that laid the foundation of Rosemary growing up to be the most fluent in Ga.

While I was expecting Henry, we heard the sad news of the death of Margot Crabbe, the sister of Michael's landlady in north London, married to Samuel Azu Crabbe. And four years later, there was the death of Ione, also from England, who was married

Difficult Days

to David Acquah. They were both social workers. Margot left young children - a daughter and a son - and Ione left a young daughter. Although neither Margot nor Ione died of a tropical disease, I realised that life anywhere, but especially in the tropics, could be quite precarious. However, Rosemary's trip to Accra gave me confidence that if anything happened to me, my children would be well looked after and happy.

Henry, Ade and Rosemary

Henry was born in January 1954 in the bungalow at Yendi. I was supposed to be going to Tamale to have him in the posh 'European' hospital but, as usual, the labour was short and Michael delivered him. He was at home because it was a public holiday. In fact we had intended going on a little picnic but I suddenly felt 'unwell'. The baby arrived a bit early probably because we had been to a party the night before and a dance at the hospital! I had been asked to dance by one of the male nurses and maybe that speeded things up.

There were some American missionaries living in a small village not too far from Yendi. We visited them once or twice. They had built themselves a very nice bungalow, and had an electric generator giving them power for lighting and all their numerous gadgets. Outside sat a row of local children watching their washing machine spinning round. To them the daily life of these Americans was almost like watching television! (Not that we had television in those days and I don't remember even having a radio.) Outside was parked an American-sized car and - a small aeroplane! The purpose of having the aeroplane was to transport seriously-ill patients to Yendi where there was an airstrip (very basic). One could land by day but not by night because there was no electricity for lights to guide the plane down.

Unfortunately most emergencies occurred in the middle of the night and the missionary (who was also a trained pilot) had to take them by road (a very bumpy ride). I think they also used the plane to go to Tamale every Saturday morning to shop! After Henry was born, they came to Yendi once by day and took Rosemary, Ade and Michael up for a spin! I was too nervous and made some excuse, holding the baby and watching. They were a nice couple with a young baby. They had had some tragedy in their life as their first child died in a road accident when they were on leave in America.

Difficult Days

Henry and Michael

Michael really enjoyed the work in Yendi and had the added interest of supervising the new hospital they were building. He was always interested in architecture as well as medicine and music. He was full of energy and sometimes on a Saturday afternoon he would gather a team of labourers and they would empty one of the soak-away pits round our bungalow. Michael had discovered that snakes were attracted to these pits. The labourers would throw all the stones out and there at the bottom would be a couple of snakes. The men would control their natural instinct to kill them quickly with rapid blows to the head, and, under Michael's direction, would flick them alive into a kerosene tin full of formalin where the poor things died. Then they would be put into a bottle and kept on display at the hospital. I wonder whether this collection of snakes is still there at Yendi Hospital.

Once I had got over the birth of Henry, I became horribly bored and horribly homesick too. I remember that Ade (who was then about twelve) was a great comfort to me. For one thing she put Henry on her back first thing in the morning before she went to school, which gave me the chance to have an extra hour's sleep. Then she was a good listener, and I would chatter on about life in England and all my relatives there and she would listen enthralled. At least it improved her command of English, which she was also keen to do. I'm afraid I was making no progress with learning to speak or understand Ga. There were several reasons for this. First of all we were in the north where Ga was not spoken. Second, the children living with us wanted to practise and improve their English. Without boasting, I can say that those who lived with us, even the domestic helpers, some of whom were illiterate, finished by speaking perfect English, which was to their advantage. Thirdly, my hearing problem made it difficult for me to hear precisely, and practise repeating, words spoken in a foreign language.

There was one very interesting character working at the Yendi hospital and that was the interpreter. He was quite elderly, and had probably been there since the hospital opened. I don't know if he had any formal qualifications, but he spoke and understood dozens of the local languages fluently. His services were indispensable, and he had a whole sheaf of glowing testimonials from the previous expatriate doctors. Michael, of course, needed his help as much as the doctors from abroad.

However, at times, he could be rather irritating, as he followed Michael everywhere like his shadow - and Michael was definitely someone who needed his own space. Also, Michael valued his relationship with the nurses and other medical staff - male and female - who were very professional with their smart uniforms and trained attitudes. He didn't want anybody usurping their important role. But nothing could alter the fact that the doctors and nurses came and went, while the interpreter was a permanent fixture!

One day at breakfast I said, 'I don't know what to do with myself, I'm so bored.' Michael replied, 'Well, today is operating day. Why don't you come down and watch?' He had a natural aptitude for surgery, and I think he wanted to show off his skills even though he knew that I understood very little about medicine. Operations were definitely not my cup of tea, but I was so desperate that I said, 'Yes, I will.'

The first operation was an amputation above the knee. Horrific! Even with my laywoman's eye I could see Michael was doing it so well and I felt proud of him. Of course the interpreter followed Michael everywhere (even though an anaesthetised patient would hardly need an interpreter!) and with scant regard for sterilization procedures. As soon as the leg was completely

The interpreter, Michael, Rosemary and myself

severed, the interpreter seized hold of it and dumped it in a bucket with the foot uppermost, and strode off with it. This was the last straw as far as I was concerned, and I quickly retreated to the anteroom, sat down and took a few deep breaths.

However I wasn't going to admit how queasy I felt. I went back to the theatre, and the next operation was a hernia. This wasn't so bad as the body was completely covered with white cloths. Once the incision was made the inside didn't look quite so human - to me at any rate. Once again everything seemed to go very smoothly and I could see that the theatre staff were really

Difficult Days

proud that one of their own people had now taken over from the expatriate doctors. There were one or two more minor procedures and I managed to survive to the end of the operating session. But I took care never to complain again that I felt bored, and I never entered the theatre again!

It was in Yendi that we made our first contact with the Canhams, an English family. Mr Canham senior was visiting his son and two daughters, all working in the Gold Coast. His son Peter was a civil servant and later became Secretary to the Cabinet, and also headmaster of a secondary school when he retired from that post. Pamela was a doctor and married to Gwyn Hughes, the geologist. Jennifer was an electrical engineer, and was responsible for the first street lights along the Ring Road in Accra. Mr Canham Senior was asked to be a Recording Officer in Yendi for the elections in 1954 after which Kwame Nkrumah was released from prison to become Prime Minister.

While in the north we also got to know Bill and Audrey Tordoff. Bill was a lecturer in Political Science, and attached to the Tamale branch of the Extra-Mural Department of the University College of the Gold Coast at Legon, just outside Accra. He was posted to Tamale to organise all sorts of classes and activities for mature students. It is true to say there were a great many English 'colonialists' who gave their services unstintingly to help build up the Gold Coast, so that there could be a smooth transition to independent Ghana.

~ *Chapter 8* ~

Two Very Different Furloughs

In 1954 it was time for Michael to go on leave. Everything was geared to the European doctors who did a tour of about eighteen months and then went to England on leave for a three-month 'furlough', as it was called. This wasn't ideal for the Gold Coast doctors but they had to fit in. We didn't think we could stay at Derby Avenue for such a long time, so we booked in at a Rest House for government servants on the outskirts of Accra and went to Derby Avenue for meals. The Rest House was only supposed to put people up for short periods so from time to time we moved from one room to another to make it appear that we were new arrivals!

Michael's mother was a really excellent cook, and I enjoyed the traditional dishes especially soup and fufu. She would put in so many different ingredients - meat, fish, salted pig's trotters ('nane'), crabs, beans, and of course tomatoes and onions, and sometimes okra and garden eggs. Some pepper was added but not too much, bearing in mind that I was not used to it. The resulting flavour was superb, and the fufu, pounded in a mortar with a long stick flattened at the end was deliciously light and full of air. But I'm afraid I never acquired a taste for the local kenkey, made from fermented corn.

Pounding fufu

While we were on leave we were invited to a meal with the then Director of Medical Services, an Englishman. I made a big mistake. Well, maybe it didn't have any effect - maybe he had already made up his mind where he was posting Michael next. However, as we were shaking hands with him as we left, I said, 'I don't mind where we go as long as we stay put for a while and don't keep moving around." Whether it was my fault or not, I don't know, but Michael's next posting, in 1954, was to the Ankaful Leprosarium where nobody else wanted to go.

So far Michael had not benefited from the system of 'private practice' mentioned earlier. In Sekondi the senior doctors had grabbed all the fee-paying patients; and in Tamale and Yendi no fees were charged in the north. Now we were being sent to a leprosarium where again treatment was free. We certainly weren't doing as well financially as many of Michael's fellow Gold Coast doctors.

However Michael enjoyed the challenge as it was different from anything he had done before. He even performed some operations much to the delight of the English nursing sister. I remember he did several that hadn't been done at Ankaful before. When the disease had caused the ulnar nerve in the upper arm to thicken, he stripped it down in order to give the leper's hands more flexibility and mobility. Of course he wasn't there long enough to follow up the long-term results, and wasn't one for writing up papers. He was always too busy. When the Leprosy Specialist went on leave, he was in charge, so he also had to do a lot of trekking, visiting the many small leprosaria that were to be found in most large towns.

Michael examining a leprosy patient

I was pregnant again but not feeling too bad this time so I did a little part-time teaching at Michael's old school Mfantsipim, while the English teacher was on leave. I drove from Ankaful to Cape Coast, taking the coastal road because a bridge along the shorter route was being repaired. I enjoyed the ride along the coast with the ever-changing sea looking so beautiful. By this time I had learnt to choose steward boys that were good with children rather than those who were good at housework. Henry was definitely hyper-active from the word go. He walked at nine months and never slept through the night. But he was a lovely, lively boy who kept everyone on their toes. Never a dull moment!

After enjoying Michael's mother's cooking, I realized I had to employ a woman to cook the traditional meals. This was a great help.

Pauline Davey with Henry fast asleep

While we were at Ankaful, we had a visitor from England, a cousin of my old friend Joyce Dudding called Pauline Davey. She enjoyed our various activities, and went with Michael when he was on trek. Then later she went to the north on her own and stayed with Elizabeth Bannerman-Richter, a relative of ours who was a nurse working in Tamale. Pauline was a scientist and while she was in Bolgatanga, she met an English doctor doing some research on malaria. Pauline helped by dissecting mosquitoes to see if there were parasites in their salivary glands. We really enjoyed her short visit.

Michael had asked for a transfer as soon as the Leprosy Specialist came back from leave, but of course we did not know where we would be going. As the time approached for the birth, I became rather nervous as I always had very quick labours, so I didn't want Michael out of my sight. He was going on trek to Tarkwa and I insisted on going with him. Rosemary and Henry came along too. When we got to Tarkwa we found that the road to the doctor's bungalow was up a very steep hill. Our car was giving quite a lot of trouble and had a habit of stalling when we changed gear. I said, 'Well, I only hope that we are not coming here!' Later we learnt from the doctor in charge, Dr Sam Otoo, that a relative of his who worked in the Ministry of Health had told him that Dr Baddoo would be taking over from him! There was a lovely view from the bungalow but I dreaded that steep hill. It was also rather irritating that someone working in the office in Accra was spreading the news of our move before we knew about it.

Back at Ankaful, Winifred arrived a little early (no doubt due to my travels) but this time I managed to get to the Cape Coast hospital in time, and had a relatively slow labour (for me anyway) and an easy delivery. The midwife was excellent. I blessed this lovely little newcomer for sparing me another alarmingly precipitate labour. I was home in time to cope with our move to

Two Very Different Furloughs

Tarkwa. Winifred was only a few weeks old, but in her usual helpful way wasn't much trouble. But our steward boy declared that Tarkwa was a wicked place and refused to come with us. Our cook was a young lady who said she would come, but when we reached Takoradi she said she had toothache and wanted to get down and go to the dentist! We knew this was just an excuse, but we let her go. Fortunately Michael's sister Elizabeth had come to help, and so we all survived.

Apart from the frighteningly steep road, the bungalow was built on stilts, and Dr Otoo's English wife, Sylvia, had warned me that some of the flooring had been declared unsafe, and we should avoid using one or two of the rooms. This was a bit worrying with two lively children and a new-born baby.

Tarkwa was a very different place from Yendi. The patients had every confidence in their own 'black' doctors, as apart from Michael's immediate predecessor Dr Otoo (Elizabeth Boi-Doe's brother), they had had the services of Dr Evans-Anfom, later to be Henry's father-in-law. Michael was extremely busy as once again he was the only doctor in charge of quite a large hospital. Every day when I sent his lunch down in a basket, he would take a break to eat it and have a short rest. He was often called out at night and then up again at seven or eight to carry on working. He seemed to thrive on it and had endless energy. When he became the choirmaster and organist at the Tarkwa Methodist Church, he decided to teach them Handel's 'Messiah'. They finished up by having a choir practice every evening. I was not too enthusiastic about being left on my own with three young children, not only all day but also every evening as well. However I could see that Michael and the choristers were enjoying the challenge, and the performance they put on at the Community Centre was well worth any sacrifice. I'm sure some of the younger members of the choir who are still alive can remember it.

The Tarkwa Methodist Church Choir

At Tarkwa, 'private practice' was allowed and this was a great help. The first thing we did was to buy a piano, and Michael's father managed to get one in Accra and bring it to Tarkwa on a lorry. I held my breath as the lorry toiled up that steep hill to the bungalow! Every month I helped Michael post bills to all sorts of

Two Very Different Furloughs

firms who sent patients to him, and of course some patients paid cash. Every month he took a third of what he had earned and shared it amongst the nurses and other staff, and the system worked very well. Most doctors earning money from 'private practice' did the same.

He even earned enough for us to go to England for our next leave. We stayed with my mother in Green Moor Link, Winchmore Hill. Michael, still intent on being a surgeon, arranged to do a course to prepare for the Primary FRCS. He surprised my mother by quickly buying carpenter's tools and wood and making himself a desk. Unfortunately he didn't pass the exam but this was nothing unusual for a first attempt. He enjoyed it and learnt a lot. It was just a pity he never had the chance to try again.

Our leave was up and we had to go back. I had enjoyed being in England, and seeing family and friends once more, especially my old friend Doreen who was working in London. My mother found the children very noisy and difficult, and went off to Worthing to stay with my sister Jean. It puzzled me then but I can understand it now that I am in my eighties! Of course she was only sixty at that time but always nervous and waiting for accidents to happen. In fact one serious accident did happen and perhaps my mother was right to think I wasn't always taking due care.

I was in the kitchen, Rosemary was playing with her friend next door, and Winifred was fast asleep upstairs. Michael had gone

Rosemary, Henry and Winifred

out to meet some Gold Coast friends in the centre of London. I was peeling potatoes and had my back to three-year-old Henry who was playing on the floor. Suddenly there was a terrific explosion. What had happened was that Henry was fiddling with the gas cooker and turned the switch to the highest level for the oven. This switch was supposed to be childproof but, clever as he is, he got round that problem. The kettle was on the gas at the back of the cooker and I knew he could not reach that so I was not worrying. The gas was gathering in the oven, and there was no pilot light in those days. Then he decided to open the oven door and the accumulated gas caught fire with a big explosion. I was horrified. His face was badly burnt. I quickly phoned Ken and he took us to the hospital. They examined him, and did not think any serious harm had been done. I was given ointment for his face and we went home.

On the way back he fell asleep and I put him to bed. My terrible fear was that his eyesight might be affected. When he woke I held a toy car in front of him and asked him what he saw. 'A car of course,' he said and I heaved a sigh of relief. His face looked dreadful for a fortnight or more, but after that healed perfectly. It was a good thing my mother had gone to Worthing. She couldn't have stood the anxiety and shock. But on the other hand, if she'd been there, it might not have happened. I certainly kept an eagle eye on Henry after that.

In some ways I was pleased to get back to the Gold Coast, as bringing up children was so much easier there than in England. Domestic help was very available and affordable. The children could play outside most of the time instead of being cooped up in the house, and one did not have to help them put on lots of warm clothes before going out in the cold weather.

~ Chapter 9 ~

The Gold Coast Becomes Independent

We went back to the Gold Coast just in time to enjoy some of the celebrations for independence on March 6th, 1957, when its name was changed to Ghana. We had never taken much interest in politics and were not too keen on Dr Kwame Nkrumah. He did not get on too well with the professionals, who considered they would take over when the British left, and he often belittled the chiefs. Nevertheless we could not help being caught up in the euphoria at that time. Of course we admired him for being a brave and charismatic leader, who had stood up to the British and gained independence for his country. He made, not only his own people, but also other Africans and African-Americans proud to be black, and have confidence in themselves.

The old Gold Coast was renamed Ghana after the ancient and powerful kingdom which used to exist in another part of West Africa. Owing to the very generous 'loss-of-career' terms given to expatriates working for the Colonial Service, there was a sudden exodus of most of the English doctors, as well as District Commissioners and other civil servants. We were all optimistic that, managing without them, the new independent Ghana would go on from strength to strength. None of us anticipated the many trials and tribulations that we would go through in the coming decades.

Michael was posted to Accra, and it was here that we employed the services of Yaro, who had worked for a German doctor called Dr Hoffman. Yaro, then in his early twenties, came from a small town called Bunkprugu, near Gambaga, in the north. He stayed with us for many years becoming a much-loved and devoted helper, who also introduced Kombia, a younger relative of his from the same town, into our household.

Michael was delighted to be working with Dr Charles Easmon, who was the first Ghanaian to qualify as a surgical specialist. He hoped this might lead to him being sent on scholarship to study for the FRCS. Unfortunately, this didn't happen. Rather, after three months he was sent to Saltpond to take charge there, and also to train some senior male nurses to become Health Centre Superintendents. He was kept pretty busy lecturing them and running the hospital single-handed.

Yaro and the children

Michael's mother had obtained a piece of land for her son, in Lartebiokorshie in Accra, so Michael wanted to start putting up a building. Michael's mother was very energetic visiting various chiefs and obtaining pieces of land. She knew that her husband was a 'royal' and heir to the chieftancy of the Sempe clan of Accra. He gave up his claim because he considered some of the chieftancy rites were incompatible with his Christian beliefs. It is interesting to note that the present Sempe Chief Nii Kwei Kuma III, is a staunch Christian. In the intervening years there have been many changes - for example, polygamy is not now a necessary part of chieftancy.

The chiefs that Sybilla, my mother-in-law, approached were only too willing to comply with her requests for pieces of land, usually with only a token fee. After the plans for a large two-storey building and a small 'outhouse' for the land at Lartebiokorshie had been drawn up, they went through the process of being passed by the various planning departments. We decided to put a wall round half of the land (which consisted of four large plots between two proposed roads), and also to start building the 'outhouse'. Almost every weekend Michael travelled to Accra to see how the contractor was getting on. I think the contractor took extra care because Michael's eagle eye was upon his work.

We knew too that any piece of land that was not built upon was liable to be taken over by unauthorized persons. If they managed to put up a building, it was very expensive to take them to court and win the case. Even if one won, the guilty party retained the building and only had to pay compensation to the rightful owners, who therefore never got the land back. This in fact happened later to one quarter of this piece of land. We should have put a wall round the whole area, but walls cost quite a lot of money.

Later that year, Karley was born at Saltpond. Once again I was supposed to be going to Cape Coast Hospital, but the labour was so quick that I didn't manage to get there. The residential area had its own generator, and every night it was turned off between 10 pm and 6 am. Of course Karley arrived in the early hours of

Michael, myself and the children

the morning at about 2 am. We managed with the help of a hurricane lamp! In the morning when Henry came wandering into our bedroom as he usually did, I said, 'Go and look in the cot.' He did so and then solemnly came back to me and lifted up the sheet to look at my tummy. He wanted to make sure that the baby had actually moved from one place to the other. I could see him working it all out in his head. I thought it was rather clever of him at the age of not quite four. Winifred at that time was two and a quarter. She was not jealous of the new baby, and was hardly ever any trouble, always happily occupied. One of her favourite activities was washing her doll's clothes, so we fixed up a clothesline a couple of feet from the ground. How she enjoyed getting each peg - with some difficulty - precisely in position! Later when they were dry, she gathered them in and ironed them with her toy iron!

It was at Saltpond that we got to know Dr Pamela Hughes and her husband, Gwyn, who was head of the Geology Department. Pamela had just had her eldest child, Peter, and she and I used to meet under some shady trees every afternoon for a chat, with Karley and Peter in their prams happily sleeping or watching the overhanging branches, swaying in the breeze.

Pamela Hughes, Michael, myself and students

While we were at Saltpond, Rosemary stayed with Emmanuel and Doris Lartey in Accra, and started going to the Ridge Church School, as she was over five. She really enjoyed it. The headmistress was an English lady, Mrs Stronge, and she made a wonderful job of running one of the first international primary schools. At that time, about fifty per cent of the children were Europeans and fifty per cent Ghanaians. The same mix was found in the Ridge Church itself. Nowadays of course, both school and church are almost one hundred per cent Ghanaians.

Again Rosemary was thrown into a Ga-speaking environment, although a lot of English was spoken as well. As she was quite young to be away from home, I made sure I picked her up every Friday for the weekend, until one weekend she said, 'Do I have to come home every weekend?' Apparently she missed all sorts of exciting activities going on at the Larteys at weekends, such as a trip to the cinema, or to the Ambassador Hotel for soft drinks.

A party at the Larteys, with Doris holding Karley

I had to rely on breastfeeding as a means of contraception, because the 'Pill' had yet to be invented, and other artificial means of contraception were not readily available in the area where we lived. Much to my horror, when Karley was about eight months old, I found I was pregnant. I decided I just could not cope with another baby, and decided to have an abortion. This was probably illegal at the time, but the Gold Coast women (and doctors) had never paid much attention to this, which was to them, an unreasonable British law.

Once Michael was sure I wanted to go ahead with it, we had no difficulty making the arrangements, but I never felt happy about what was, after all, against all my principles. I took a long time recovering both physically and psychologically. Michael knew how distressed I was and the box containing the precious 'pedal attachments' for the piano, which would enable him to practise organ music at home, using both hands and feet, stood unopened for a long time. They had of course been specially ordered from England after Michael had sent them a detailed plan of the strings of our particular make of piano. At any other time he would not have been able to wait to get them fixed and I appreciated his sensitivity.

In October 1958, we had another visitor from England, Doreen Sear (now Doreen Page). During our brief stay in Accra when I had met Dr Silas Dodu and his English wife, Joan, I had envied Joan having her mother to stay. I had always longed to have a member of the family see me in my new setting and perhaps give me praise for how well I was coping. At the same time, I knew it was highly unlikely that my mother would ever get on a plane and visit West Africa, and of course my brothers and sisters were busy bringing up their own children. Lily might have considered coming if her health had been better, and I remember Ken's son Richard hoping his ship might arrive in Ghana when he was doing his National Service in the Navy, but it never did.

Silas and Joan Dodu, with Densua and Namua

Having Doreen to stay was a great joy. She bought a cine camera and lots of films before coming and took to film making like a duck to water. Looking back, we did not do anything terribly exciting but just followed our normal routine with the children and social activities. Maybe we should have been more adventurous and taken her to Kumasi and Tamale to see more of the country's culture and heritage. However, Michael was working, and I was also doing some teaching at Wesley Girls' High School, so we could not go far afield.

Doreen was pleased to accompany Michael occasionally on his visits to the various rural clinics - as well as going to school with me sometimes! It was the season for school Speech Days too and she enjoyed attending the Mfantsipim Founders' Day celebrations, and their special Church Service in Cape Coast. We also went to the Wesley Girls' High School Speech Day, meeting some of the girls and members of staff, including the Headmistress Miss Compton and our dear Clarice Garnett who was later to succeed her. The speaker for the day was Mr Robert Gardiner, whom she vividly remembered hearing some years previously giving an address in England.

Of course we took her to Accra once or twice where we were welcomed and entertained by Michael's family at Derby Avenue, and also visited the Lartey family, and the Ridge Church School as well as attending morning service at Wesley Church. Another great attraction for her was Ghana's beautiful and interesting coastline. We had a splendid view of the sea from our bungalow at Saltpond, and she managed to coax us all out into the garden

The Gold Coast Becomes Independent

(even Michael sometimes!). Before her visit, we had adopted the Ghanaian habit of escaping out of the sun instead of revelling in it. With her encouragement, we all enjoyed the sun and the scenery from the stoep, one such occasion being Karley's first birthday.

Further afield, as well as Cape Coast, we visited Ankaful, and some of the other castles along the coast. There were picnics on the beach at Biriwa where, on one occasion, we were joined by the Becketts, a young couple on the staff at Mfantsipim School, Cape Coast, whom Doreen had got to know during the voyage out on the APAPA. We also went to some Harvest Festivals in the rural areas round Saltpond, and the welcome we got was heart-warming. I think Doreen really enjoyed her visit, coming by sea and returning by air. She was sad when it was time to go home and we were sorry to see her leave. Subsequently I found writing letters to someone who knew the background so much easier.

Our 'tour' of duty came to an end. All Michael's students passed except one who was a known heavy drinker! We went on leave and this time stayed with the Larteys. This was another opportunity to experience the Ghanaian way of life. Emmanuel, a relative of Michael's on his father's side, was Chief Engineer for the Accra City Council. Doris, his wife, was from Ada where they spoke Dangme, a dialect of Ga. They lived in a government bungalow so life was quite different from the traditional family house in Derby Avenue, but still very Ghanaian. Doris was not working full-time but gave talks on the radio on women's affairs and childcare. She also had a beautiful voice and was often asked to sing solos in various churches. The children were Joy (later Mrs Ashong) who was about nine, Victor, about six, and Emmanuel (later a Methodist minister) about four.

After our leave we were asked to go to Sekondi-Takoradi again, and of course we took Rosemary with us this time as there were suitable 'international' schools there. The term 'international' seemed to be tacked on to all private primary schools even if all the children were Ghanaians! It simply meant that fees were paid and that all the classes were in English! Michael was asked to take charge of the Out-Patients and the Maternity Departments. Again, the latter was a new field for him. He really did have a very broad career, which stood him in good stead when he became Director of Medical Services.

While we were there arrangements were being made for the wedding of Michael's third sister, Victoria, to Victor Akushie. I had by this time realized that these social gatherings meant a great deal to all Ghanaians. This applied chiefly to funerals, but also to weddings and 'outdoorings', traditional marriages and significant birthdays such as one's 50th or 80th. It seems that in the so-called 'third world' people depend more on the community for support. Instead of going for an expensive holiday where one gets away from it all, the people spend what seems like a lot of money gathering their extended family and friends round them, dressing and feasting as extravagantly as possible. There was also a certain element of 'one-upmanship' as one tried to do as well, if not better, than one's neighbours.

When we were in Tarkwa, I had met a Scotswoman from Aberdeen, called Jeanne, who was married to a friend of Michael's, Kofi Amonoo, a geologist. They were now at Sekondi-Takoradi, and with her help and encouragement, I rustled up some really nice outfits for myself and the children to wear at this important wedding. Men's clothes were never a problem as long as they had an English-style suit, which of course was terribly hot in the tropics but nobody seemed to mind that. Jeanne was to become a close friend, even though we were often living far apart.

We all went off to Accra, proud to be able to stay in our new building at Lartebiokorshie. We even had some furniture - beds and sitting-room chairs. Unfortunately, there were no wardrobes or even shelves. I had always been very careful putting drugs high out of reach of the children. On this occasion, I must have left the tablets of the malaria prophylactic, Daraprim, in our travelling case. The next afternoon I went off to have my hair done for the wedding, leaving Yaro, and our niece Ade, then sixteen, in charge of the four children - quite a handful!

Somehow Karley, then nearly two, got hold of the Daraprim tablets and chewed them up. She started having convulsions, and Yaro, with great presence of mind, wrapped her in a blanket and ran all the way from the Lartebiokorshie house to the main road to get (with difficulty) a taxi to the Korle Bu hospital, which was about three kilometres away. She was given expert treatment, and after spending a night in hospital, quickly recovered. The rest of us went to the wedding in order not to disappoint Victoria, who has always been one of my favourite sisters-in-law. Another near tragedy! At least this drove all thoughts of 'guilt' about the abortion right out of my mind.

~ Chapter 10 ~

Life at Korle Bu

After our leave spent in our house at Lartebiokorshie, Michael was asked to take over as Medical Superintendent at Korle Bu Hospital. It was now clear that his hopes of doing surgery were dashed and he was being pushed into administration. He took it philosophically but deep-down it was a great disappointment. However, he enjoyed his new post in many ways because he sympathized with people, not only patients but also staff. We lived in one of the old-fashioned bungalows on stilts at the lower end of Slater Avenue.

I greatly enjoyed being in a place where there were lots of other wives of doctors. Quite naturally I found it comforting comparing notes with the English wives of Ghanaians as we had a lot in common. I remember Joan Dodu and Nora Saakwa-Mante as well as Sheila Amoah, herself a doctor, and Leonora Evans-Anfom, who was an African American who had been to university in Edinburgh. Little did I suspect at that time that she was the mother of my 'daughter-in-law elect'! Many of us sent our children to the same school - the Ridge Church School.

Early in 1960, Michael was asked to go and do the Diploma of Public Health Course in London. I very much wanted us to be based in Winchmore Hill among familiar places and relatives and friends. Lily made efforts to find us somewhere to live, but it was Doreen Sear who finally succeeded in finding a house to rent in Myddelton Gardens, a turning off Green Dragon Lane. I really was on home ground. Just down the road was one of my late father's butcher shops and Lily was the cashier there. She always made sure I got the best cuts of meat!

When we arrived the children's ages were, as Henry was quick to point out, 2 (Karley), 4 (Winifred), 6 (Henry) and 8 (Rosemary). Very neat! Next door was a very friendly family - the Parkers with three children of similar ages. The children often all played together. Once again, little did I realize that we would keep up with the eldest child, Ann, and that more than 40 years later she and her husband would be inviting Henry's eldest daughter (then at Bristol University) to their house in the Cotswolds.

Rosemary and Henry were able to go to the local primary school and the headmistress was Margaret Booker, an old friend from the Winchmore Methodist Church. We quickly bought warm clothes and everything seemed to be running smoothly. Michael soon joined the choir at the Winchmore Hill Methodist Church, and the children went to the Sunday School. I only wanted my Mum to visit from Worthing, but she kept putting off her visit.

Our tenth wedding anniversary came round in May and we went off to the theatre in the West End to see the opera 'Aida', while Doreen looked after the children. It was a wonderful experience, and I realized how much we were missing living in Ghana. I looked forward to a year of good things, not knowing there were going to be a few problems too.

That summer we went on holiday to Woolacombe in Devon with Doreen. Michael was still busy on his course, but came down at the weekend. This was a new experience for the children - an ordinary English seaside holiday, playing on the beach, digging sand castles and dipping into the sea. Winifred celebrated her fifth birthday while we were there. Back in London once more for the autumn term, Winifred joined her brother and sister at school, leaving only Karley at home. It happened that Jeanne and Kofi Amonoo and their two daughters were living in Southgate - not far off - so we met quite frequently. Often Michael would go off on Saturday or Sunday, taking Rosemary with him, to enjoy meeting Ghanaians living in other parts of London. We were all happily enjoying ourselves.

Finally Mum arrived and I could immediately see that she was in a very nervous state. She soon had to be admitted to the Friern

Clare Parker, Winifred, Michele Amonoo, Karley and Carmen Amonoo

Barnet Psychiatric Hospital and treated for an obsessive-compulsive disorder. This was quite a shock for us all, and for the rest of her life she was in and out of hospitals. Often the various treatments seemed successful, but her recovery did not last. At the time of her first admission I visited her as much as possible. On one occasion I remember coming home and lying on the sofa silently weeping. One of the children - I can't remember who - rushed over and vainly tried to push the tears running down my cheeks back into my eyes! I couldn't help smiling.

Life at Korle Bu

Once again I was pregnant - we seemed to be taking the biblical injunction 'Be fruitful and multiply' a little too seriously! Soon after Christmas I had a miscarriage and was in hospital myself for a week or so.

I recovered in time for Easter when we were invited by Sir Geoffrey Keynes, the surgeon, and his wife Lady Keynes, to Lammas House near Newmarket for the weekend. Michael had often worked on his 'firm' at Barts when he was a student. Sir Geoffrey invited him home on several occasions and had taken a friendly interest in his career. We took with us Rosemary and Henry and I just hoped they would be on their best behaviour. Once more Doreen stepped into the breach and looked after Winifred and Karley. The weekend didn't start off very well when I mispronounced their name ('Keens' instead of 'Canes' - pronunciation has never been my strong point!) and was roundly corrected by the formidable Lady Keynes. Then on Sunday morning a few of the Keynes' relatives arrived with their children and there was the traditional Easter egg hunt in the garden. Their children were rather younger than ours, and I was embarrassed when Henry, always enjoying a competitive race, rushed round gathering up every egg in sight instead of holding back and letting his host's children find at least a few of them.

That summer Doreen took Michael and Rosemary on a day trip to France - another new and enjoyable experience for both of them, except that Michael nearly passed out in the 'tropical' heatwave that day ('It's never as hot as this in Ghana!'). We had so many enjoyable times as well as the stressful problems that had unexpectedly cropped up. The children were doing well at school, and even had a few music lessons on the piano. Michael successfully completed his course.

Soon afterwards, unfortunately, he became ill with a duodenal ulcer! Really our stay in England was a mixture of pleasant and unpleasant experiences! Like many doctors, he made a very difficult patient, and imagined that he had all sorts of other diseases apart from the fairly straightforward ulcer! When he recovered, our stay in England came to an end and we returned to Ghana. Michael went first with Rosemary and Henry by ship. I wanted to see a bit more of my mother who was now at Graylingwell Hospital in Worthing. I followed later by air with Winifred and Karley. I must say that once more I was pleased to return to Ghana. In September 1961, as soon as Michael was busy as Medical Superintendent of Korle Bu and the Accra Group of Hospitals, he forgot all about his worries about himself and thoroughly enjoyed the job.

It was quite a difficult situation with the setting up of the Medical School. Some of the staff at Korle Bu were employed by the Ministry of Health, and some were under the Medical School which was part of the University of Ghana at Legon, and of course they had more favourable salaries and conditions of service. Originally the plan had been to build a separate Medical

School Hospital and this might had avoided some of the inevitable friction between the two groups.

Politically Nkrumah became more and more powerful, calling himself 'Osagyefo' and making himself Life President of a one-party state. Every morning as I drove the children to school I had to pass his statue with the inscription underneath, 'Seek ye first the political kingdom, and all else shall be added unto you,' which I thought quite blasphemous, and which put me in a bad mood for the rest of the day. The children were enjoying themselves at the Ridge Church School, where there were European and African children in almost equal numbers. After assembly the European children went back to their classrooms, while the Ghanaian children grouped themselves round the flag and recited the pledge - 'I promise on my honour to be faithful and loyal to Ghana, my motherland. I pledge myself to the service of Ghana with all my strength and with all my heart. I promise to hold in high esteem our heritage, won for us through the blood and toil of our fathers; and I pledge myself in all things to uphold and defend the good name of Ghana. So help me God.'

This was compulsory in the government schools and Mrs Stronge wisely decided it should be done at the Ridge Church School. One day at home this conversation took place between myself and the children -

Me: Do you go and recite the pledge after assembly?
Children: (in a Chorus) Of course!
Me: What I mean is, are you English or Ghanaian?
Children: (Chorus) Ghanaian, of course!!!
Me: Oh, I see. Well, so what am I then?
Children: (Chorus) You're half-Ghanaian!!

I was quite pleased with the firmness of their answers. They knew exactly where they stood - no identity crisis for them. And I felt I wasn't doing too badly as a half-Ghanaian in spite of being unable to pick up more than a smattering of the Ga language. Whatever the children decided to do or where they decided to live and work when they were adults, I felt that as they were living in Ghana as children they might as well come down firmly on the Ghanaian side of their inheritance. It is interesting to see how, decades later, my grandchildren living in England are encouraged to come down firmly on the English side of their inheritance. Very wise, I think.

The wives of the doctors at Korle Bu all got together and organized various activities. We were now living at 5 Harley Street, a large two-storeyed house (but still called a 'bungalow' because it was a government building!) with an extensive garden. I remember organizing a Sports Day, which all the children at Korle Bu enjoyed.

Life at Korle Bu

Later I set up Sunday School classes because the bridge over the Korle lagoon was being rebuilt and for a couple of years it was a longer journey to the Ridge Church. The numbers grew and we moved to the Catering Rest House where there was more room, and finally to the Nurses' Training College. By this time I had several Christian Fellowship Ghanaian helpers who eventually took it over very successfully, when it became too much for me to organize.

I also arranged piano lessons at our bungalow. I advertised for a piano teacher, and who should turn up one day but an Englishman named Reg Brookes. He had been a pilot in the Second World War and had been shot down and sustained serious injuries. His face had been badly burnt and he had lost several of his fingers or parts of them. He benefited from plastic surgery, which was making rapid strides to meet the needs of the those injured in war. Reg never made much of the terrible time he had been through, and wasn't the least bit embarrassed by his ravaged looks. He came every week and taught our children and several other children living at Korle Bu. He had settled in Accra because the warm climate made his injuries easier to bear, and he ran a night-club there. He played beautifully on the piano in spite of disabilities, and obviously would have become a brilliant pianist had he not been injured, but he never complained.

In December 1962, I heard the sad news that my sister Jean had died. I felt very sorry that I was so far away and unable to help. But at least her two children Sheila and Kenneth were older now and better able to cope with their bereavement. Some time later, Jack, who had devotedly cared for his wife throughout her illness, remarried. His second wife, Stella, was a very caring woman who sensitively devoted herself to bringing comfort and hope back to Jack's life, and also gave a lot of support to her two not-so-young stepchildren.

By this time I was expecting again and quite pleased to look forward to an addition to the family after my two losses. Some of my friends were not so sure. One told me she thought I was making a big mistake, and four children were quite enough! This made me very angry as I was six months pregnant at the time and such a remark was uncalled for (even if that was her opinion). She has now passed on, and never lived to see how well my 'big mistake' is doing, and how he is helping to look after me in my old age. While I was waiting for the baby to arrive, I just hoped it would be a boy as Henry threatened to leave home if it was another girl. He really was fed-up with all their girlish activities such as ballet-dancing lessons run by Rene Attoh, a retired dancer and trapeze artiste from the Netherlands, married to a Ghanaian. Jimmy arrived on a Sunday, the day after the Homowo festival on the Saturday. Everybody was delighted.

None of the other children had been born in Accra and therefore none of them had undergone the traditional naming ceremony called 'Kpodzemo' (outdooring) or 'Gbei woo' (naming ceremony) performed when the baby is one week old. As this was likely to be my last child, Michael's family was determined that this ceremony would take place. It had to be performed at Michael's family house in Derby Avenue and before the last star had left the sky shortly before dawn. Long before this I was up and dressed to go with the baby. My sisters-in-law said I could stay and rest, and they would take the baby and bring him safely back afterwards, but I was determined to be there. I had never attended an outdooring before as we had been out of Accra most of the time. I was a bit apprehensive about what was actually going to be done to my very tiny, and precious, baby.

The ceremony took place in the courtyard, and neither I nor Michael were supposed to be present. However, we watched from an upstairs window, as the baby was put into the arms of a respected male member of the family, in this case, Michael's father, whose first name was 'James'. He gained the people's attention by saying, 'Tswa, tswa, tswa!' followed by, 'Omaney aba!' (meaning 'Let goodness come!') with the gathered people responding 'Yaoo!' in affirmation. Then the baby was laid naked on the bare ground to symbolize that he must accept the harsh realities of life. After that the baby was given three drops of water, then three drops of rum (or other alcoholic drink) and told, 'If it is water, say it is water; if it is rum, say it is rum,' to symbolize the importance of telling the truth. Then he was given his name - 'Akwei'. To everything my father-in-law said at this important

Winifred, the future paediatrician, with Jimmy

ceremony, the people firmly responded, 'Yaoo!'

His full name on the birth certificate is Geoffrey James Akwei Baddoo, as he was also named after Sir Geoffrey Keynes. In the years that followed, I attended several outdoorings, and always found them very moving. By the time the ceremony ended, dawn had broken and refreshments were served to all those present. The atmosphere at the naming of our second son, Akwei, (although he was always known as Jimmy at first, and then Jim) became that of a party. However, as it was a Sunday, most people had to slip away in order not to be late for church.

~ *Chapter 11* ~

Busy with Our Five Children

A month after Jimmy was born, Rosemary, after doing well in the Common Entrance Exam, went to Achimota School just outside Accra, boarding in Slessor House. I had never been to boarding school myself, but it was obviously the normal thing in Ghana, and once again I thought it would be good for the children to conform to the Ghanaian way of life. They certainly all did well at boarding school and made some life-long friends.

Meanwhile, we had made friends with Dr David and Mrs Moira Murray. David was the doctor in charge of Achimota Hospital, which catered for the needs of the students, the staff and their families, and the people living in the surrounding villages. It was reassuring to know that Moira was very friendly with the mainly English staff, and she could easily alert me if Rosemary was unhappy or if there were any problems. As it was, she settled down very well, especially as we were able to visit almost every weekend, always taking some food, of course!

Soon after this, I decided to get a job as English Tutor at the Nurses' Training College. At that time, they had a Pre-Nursing Course to get students up to scratch in English and Science before they trained as State Registered Nurses. I started working part-time and then quickly switched to full-time work because I knew Jimmy was in Yaro's safe hands. Meanwhile Michael was enjoying work as the Medical Superintendent of Korle Bu, and also enjoying being an organist at Wesley Church. He particularly enjoyed teaching the choir new anthems. He usually had only one copy of the anthem, of course in staff notation, and most of them could only sight-read from tonic sol-fa. Therefore he had to laboriously type all the parts on to a stencil in tonic sol-fa, and a member of the choir would run off 50 or 60 copies on a duplicating machine.

The next year, on February 2nd 1965, sadly Michael's father died. It was my first experience of being involved in a funeral within the family in Ghana. The final funeral rites and the wake-keeping took place at Emmanuel Inn, because when my father-in-law lost his father at a very early age he was looked after by Mr Osabutey of Emmanuel Inn. The body was laid in state on a beautifully decorated bed and I found sitting there all night a very peaceful experience and one that I shall long remember. He was a highly respected member of the community and had been organist at both Wesley Church and Freeman Memorial Chapel in Bukom Square. He had also been Secretary of Sunday Schools in Accra. So many choirs and church groups sang and came to pay their final respects. Gradually at about midnight, most of the mourners went home, and the close relatives remained till dawn. Later that morning the funeral service took place at Wesley Church.

Soon after this, in 1965, Michael was transferred to the Ministry of Health Headquarters. Nkrumah was still in power, and in that year the second meeting of the OAU (Organisation of African Unity) was held in Accra. We were invited to a few of the events held at the recently built State House. I remember hearing the famous black South African singer Miriam Makeba. She had been preceded by a rather third-rate European nightclub singer, who used all the tricks of her trade to titillate the audience. The applause was polite but muted. Then Miriam came on the stage dressed in a long flowing gown, wearing hardly any make-up, and with her usual simple 'Afro' hair-style, and started singing. It sounded so simple, but the effect was magical. The rhythms were so African, and her body moved in a subtle way. When she finished, there was a moment or two of silence before the deafening applause broke out, and she had to sing again — the audience just would not let her go.

The next one to go off to boarding school, in September 1965, was Henry, and he followed in his father's footsteps and went to Mfantsipim. The boys' schools were altogether tougher than the girls' schools and Achimota, which was mixed. He was very homesick and begged to be allowed to leave. I would have let him do so, but his Dad said 'No' and he managed to survive! He had a lot of support from his close friend and distant cousin, Emmanuel Lartey, who went at the same time. We visited as much as we could, but Cape Coast was 150 kilometres away. However I enjoyed the trips because for the journey I had Michael all to myself, which rarely happened at home, with the hospital and the choir clamouring for his attention, and the children, relatives and domestic helpers always being around. Mr J. W. Abruquah was the Headmaster at the time - an excellent man, who knew we were worried about Henry and kept an eye on him.

It was at this time that Mfantsipim were lucky enough to have Joe de Graft on their staff as a drama specialist. Before his arrival, every year at the Speech Day celebrations the boys acted a Shakespeare play. It was quite a struggle for them, and quite an endurance test for the audience. After all, we had sat through some long speeches already! Joe de Graft quickly changed all that. He put on plays by West African dramatists like 'The Lion and the Jewel' by Wole Soyinka, which were full of drumming and dancing and local culture. We all enjoyed the change! To his credit Kwame Nkrumah did everything he could to encourage Ghanaian writers, artists and musicians.

The following year in 1966, there was a military coup while Nkrumah was in China, and amid much rejoicing he was overthrown. We were living in Reindorf Avenue still in the Korle Bu hospital compound, and there were some nurses' flats opposite. We watched as the nurses came out on to their verandahs dancing with joy. Nkrumah was a great man, but unfortunately at home he had caused too much distress with measures like the Preventive Detention Act, which meant that people who opposed him could be imprisoned indefinitely without trial. We were also pleased later when Lieutenant-General Ankrah, a personal friend of ours, was made Chairman of the NLC (National Liberation Council), even though he had not taken part in the coup. It was interesting to note how quickly the children learnt the word 'coup'.

Soon after this, in 1967, Winifred went to Achimota. With three of them away from home most of the time, I took the opportunity, in the summer of '68, to go on a visit with Karley to England. We went by sea, which I always loved, but unfortunately Karley was horribly seasick. We spent some time with Doreen who had married Tom Page on the 31st of March 1964, and they were living in Carbrooke in Norfolk. She had previously been working in the centre of London for the En Famille Agency, which specialized in placing continental visitors in English homes for holidays, and vice versa. She was very happy in her dramatically changed life-style, and as both of them took early retirement, they went on lots of holidays abroad together. We all rejoiced at their good fortune, and at our good fortune in being able to spend many happy times in their Norfolk home.

The five children

While Karley and I were away, Michael, with Yaro's help, looked after Jimmy, who apparently never asked where I was or when I was coming back! Karley and I also travelled to Stockport in Cheshire, where Flora, my sister-in-law, was doing a course in paediatric nursing. She was living with an English family, the Higginbothams, and we were able to attend her wedding to Arthur

Sackeyfio, who was doing a course in Pharmacology. Karley was one of the bridesmaids, and it was a very happy occasion with the members of the Heaton Moor Methodist Church making us all very welcome.

When I went back to Ghana, I realized that the students at the Nurses' Training College had a natural talent for drama. We happened to be reading 'She Stoops to Conquer' by Oliver Goldsmith - a rather old-fashioned book with little appeal, one would think, for Ghanaian girls. I chose it because it was one of the few sets of books in the cupboard! However I decided to let the girls act the play.

Nurses at the NTC

In the original play, Mr Hardcastle hopes his daughter will marry Sir Charles Marlowe, who is visiting them as Kate's suitor.

Marlowe is always terribly shy and formal in the presence of ladies of his own social standing, but witty and flirtatious when talking to girls from the lower orders. I changed the setting to Accra, and Kate, the heroine, wore European dress and a wig (all the rage in 1966) when Marlowe was supposed to be wooing her, and traditional 'cloth' and plaited hair when she was pretending to be the maid. Naturally Marlowe fell in love with the maid! I altered a lot of the names of people and places and a lot of the dialogue to fit the Ghanaian background and even brought in a reference to General Ankrah. It went down very well, and I was pleased with my efforts.

At that time there was a World Health Organisation (WHO) Consultant in Nursing, Miss Kay Dier, a Canadian, at the Nurses' Training College, and she took a great interest in everything that was going on. She even took a couple of the staff round Accra in her car, putting up posters advertising the performances! I'm sure it was she who started the coffee club every morning when members of the staff met during their morning break. Everybody liked her and the way she went about helping change the curriculum from the rather narrow British one to a broader 'comprehensive' one which included midwifery and psychiatry in the basic course. The Canadians were well liked in Ghana. They had the happy knack of giving help quietly and unobtrusively and handing things over to Ghanaians at the earliest opportunity.

Nursing tutors including Kay Dier (centre)

Michael had a busy time at the Ministry Headquarters, and often went on trips abroad, especially to Geneva for WHO meetings. I was still working at the Nurses' Training College, enjoying producing other plays, this time by African authors. Sometimes we performed them at the Accra Community Centre. I vividly remember one occasion when the nursing students were leaving the Centre after a rehearsal. It just happened that Mrs Attoh's girls were busily practising their ballet dancing. By this time of course none of my daughters was in her classes. One of my students said scornfully, snapping her fingers, 'I don't give a ha'penny for THAT sort of dancing!' I was taken aback, partly by the use of the expression 'ha'penny', and by the fact that she spoke rather loudly in English, instead of sotto voce in the vernacular to her friends. She obviously wanted me to hear! Of course the young children weren't performing at any high level, but I was rather cross. I thought, 'She might change her view if she saw a Sadler Wells ballet at Covent Garden theatre!'

In 1969, out of the blue, Michael was suddenly transferred to Ho as the Regional Medical Officer of Health. This could hardly be regarded as a promotion! Could it be that certain people wanted him out of the way as far as being in line for promotions at Headquarters, and also enjoying all the perks of trips abroad?

Once again, Michael took it philosophically and off we went, but I was furious. I felt we had done our share of moving around. The older children were not so much affected by the move, as Rosemary had taken her O-levels and had gone to do her A-levels at the University of Science and Technology, Kumasi; Henry was at Mfantsipim; and Winifred was at Achimota. They all enjoyed the new experience of being in the Volta Region for their holidays. Karley went to the Ho International School for two terms, before going to Wesley Girls' High School in Cape Coast.

Jimmy also went to the International School at Ho, and I taught at OLA (Our Lady of the Apostles), a Catholic girls' secondary school. There, no doubt due to my anger with some features of life in Ghana, I produced a very English play called 'The Tinder Box' based on an English fairy tale. In spite of the general 'niceness' of the Ghanaian people, there were (or are?) certain aspects of their character and culture which were very negative. When anyone was doing well and popular with fellow

Winifred, Karley and Henry in Ho

workers, and enjoying a few 'perks', others became jealous and tried to 'pull him down'. This is popularly known as the 'PhD syndrome'.

After some time, I could see that Winifred was not very happy at Achimota, and this time decided to do something about it. Her handwriting was getting smaller and smaller (and exceedingly neat), and to me this meant she was not as carefree and happy as a child of her age should be! The children always teased me about the many 'theories' I held! 'Listen to Mum's theory number one thousand, seven hundred and sixty three!' one of them would exclaim. Miss Garnett, the headmistress at Wesley Girls', willingly accepted the transfer, in 1970, and Winifred (in Form 4) joined Karley (in Form 2) there and was much happier, and her handwriting resumed its big and bold characteristic!

Now that four of them were away from home, I fell into the habit of writing a weekly letter to all of them. I used the typewriter with four plain sheets of paper interspersed with three sheets of carbon paper, and happily typed the first few identical paragraphs. Then removing the sheets, I added a personal paragraph to each one. Now, 35 years later, I am doing the same sort of thing but with emails instead of carbon paper and stamps! Grandchildren have been added to the list of recipients. Things have moved on, and with a computer I have tried to keep up.

Although our move to Ho was not welcome, two things happened which made the transfer worthwhile. First of all, Michael was asked to go and do a three-month course at Johns Hopkins University in America on Health Planning. I did not enjoy his absence with only young Jimmy for company. He spent most of his time with the Benbows, a nice African-American family who lived down the road. At night, we slept in the end bedroom with all doors well locked. As the bungalow was built on a slope, this end bedroom was not on the ground floor - underneath was a garage and large storeroom, and I felt safer. Although I was kept busy at OLA school, I was really relieved when Michael returned.

Busy with Our Five Children

The second thing that happened was that there was, after Michael's return, an outbreak of cholera - the very first in Ghana. A man from the Volta region died of cholera in the neighbouring country of Togo, and his body was brought by canoe to his home town of Battor for burial. Because of the burial rites, several people contracted the disease and it quickly spread. Michael and his staff at the regional office set to work to control the outbreak. They always visited the affected areas as a team - usually Michael and the Regional Matron and the Regional Pharmacist. Later I helped Michael compile the figures and the Volta Region compared very favourably with all the other regions. Michael showed everyone that, although he might not have been blessed (or otherwise) with the 'gift of the gab', he was extremely competent in dealing with health problems at the grassroots level.

While we were in Ho, too, the NLC (National Liberation Council) held elections. The Progress Party won and Dr Kofi Abrefa Busia became Prime Minister. Although as Methodists we might be expected to support Busia as he was not only a very learned academic but also a Methodist local preacher, we found some of his policies unacceptable. First of all he expelled all the aliens (mostly Nigerians) living in Ghana, and many of them had been born there and never lived abroad at all.

Then he sacked 568 civil servants. This was popularly known as 'Apollo 568' after the eye disease spreading all over Ghana, which coincided with the journey into space of Apollo 11. No doubt some of them deserved being dismissed but certainly not two people we knew - Mr Abruquah the Headmaster of Mfantsipim, and Mr David Acquah, the Sociologist. Busia also wanted to enter into a dialogue with South Africa (still practicing apartheid), which we all thought was utter madness. On the other hand, he was very keen on improving the rural areas, and might have done much to stem the rural-urban migration, if he had stayed in power.

His period of office was short and in 1972 he was overthrown by another coup, again when Busia was out of the country. The new Military Head of State was Col. Acheampong, the Chairman of the National Redemption Council.

~ *Chapter 12* ~

Back to Accra

In 1971, Michael was suddenly called back to Accra as the Regional Medical Officer of Health for the Accra Region. Strangely enough we were travelling to Accra in our car on May 20th, our 21st wedding anniversary. As we went along we counted up the number of houses we had lived in since we married and it came to twenty-one! Quite remarkable! We were allocated a bungalow in City Corner in the centre of Accra. Michael was particularly delighted to be back with his beloved choir at Wesley Church. I went back to the Nurses' Training College, and enjoyed working with the other English Tutor, who was a Ghanaian, Miss Evelyn Anyane-Yeboah (later Mrs de Souza). We took turns, each producing a play alternate years, so I had a little more time to do other things. Jimmy went to the Ridge

Church School, and the rest were at boarding schools and university.

We were living very near the British Council, with its extensive library upstairs, and a big hall, and nice little café downstairs. The latest films were shown, and series like 'The Ascent of Man' and 'Civilisation'. There was always something going on, and a nice group of English people running it. One of them was Stella Smethurst, who had previously worked with our friend Doreen Sear at the En Famille Agency in London. What a coincidence! She quickly became a good friend. She went to the beach almost every Saturday and often took Jimmy with her. The wife of one member of staff, Mrs Reeves, gave piano lessons and I asked her to take Jimmy on as one of her pupils. Altogether life was very enjoyable.

When Busia was overthrown on January 13th 1972 and the National Redemption Council under Colonel I. K. Acheampong took over, our feelings were very mixed. We did not like many of Busia's policies, but we liked military coups even less. At first things didn't seem too bad with the emphasis on Self-Reliance, and the fine manly Colonel Bernasko leading the 'Operation Feed Yourself Programme'. People's idea of farming being only suitable for illiterates was completely shattered, and well-educated people started thinking of it as a respectable career.

Sunday afternoon guests – Ann (nee Parker) and Steve far left

It was about this time that Michael was called back to Ministry Headquarters, first as Deputy Director of Medical Services, and then as Director. He got on quite well with the three Commissioners for Health that he had to work under - Colonel Adjetey who was a Dental Surgeon; Major Selormey; and finally Lt/Col. Odartey-Wellington. Michael often appeared on television visiting hospitals and health centres with army personnel. They would be taking military strides, and poor Michael would be struggling to keep up - he had a very painful corn on the sole of one foot! But things did get done.

At that time, too, when the Medical and Dental Council and the Ghana Nurses' and Midwives Council were being set up, and the Ghana Medical Association was becoming stronger, the

Director's powers were gradually cut down. Michael was the right man for the job, as he never believed in hanging on to power for its own sake. He was also a strong believer in decentralization, and willingly handed over more responsibility to the Regional Medical Officers of Health. Of course, we had to do quite a lot of entertaining, and I was very fortunate to have my sister-in-law Comfort, to help me prepare some delicious buffet suppers.

Rosemary was quietly getting on with her course in architecture, and making a lot of friends at 'TECH'. Her chief hobby was dressmaking, which demands, I suppose, three-dimensional skills just as much as architecture! She turned out some lovely dresses for herself and other people. I remember Nana Konadu Agyeman (later Nana Konadu Agyeman Rawlings, the first lady) coming with Rosemary one morning to sew a dress needed that very afternoon for a friend's wedding!

Henry, to our delight, opted to do medicine and entered the medical school at Korle Bu with excellent A-level grades. He had already proved his interest in medicine when as Dispensary Prefect at Mfantsipim, he endeared himself to all the sick, especially the lonely, homesick Form 1 boys. He knew exactly how they felt! In 1972, Winifred was due to start her sixth form course, and Doreen Page suggested she did it in England. She was accepted at the Norwich High School for Girls and stayed with Mr and Mrs Pollock as a weekly boarder, going to Carbrooke at weekends. It was a wonderful opportunity for her.

Winifred with Doreen and Tom Page

In 1972, before Henry went to medical school, he went on a visit to England, staying with my cousin Dennis Savage and his wife Winifred. Dennis was the son of Auntie Edie and Uncle Fred, whom I had stayed with as a student. It was lovely to renew contact with this branch of the family. Henry had an interesting time in England and met up with his sister Winifred who was there for her two-year sixth form course. They visited other members of my family, and did a bit of sight-seeing.

Henry was also invited by Betty (nee Thackeray) and Alan Saunders, who lived in Hertfordshire (and whom I had known at school), to go on holiday with them in Devon, with their children

- Peter, Chris, Mark and Marion - as well as some family friends. This was quite a new experience for him as Ghanaians (at that time - perhaps things have changed now) were not used to going away on holiday. He thoroughly enjoyed the carefree and relaxed atmosphere with plenty of fun and laughter, and as he later said, 'One could be oneself, and laugh at oneself without feeling embarrassed or offended.'

In 1973, Jimmy (aged 10) and I went on a visit to England. He had never been before, and complained bitterly that it 'wasn't fair' that the rest of the family had been many times and himself not once. While there we helped Winifred celebrate her eighteenth birthday. The next year, after taking her A-levels, she returned to Ghana, hoping to join Henry at the medical school. Unfortunately, although she had reasonably good results, they did not exactly fit the entry requirements in Ghana, and she didn't get in. Michael wouldn't go against his principles and use his position to influence the selection panel. I was rather cross!

Winifred took it philosophically and went to 'extra classes' to repeat Chemistry and sit Biology and the General Paper. Most of the classes were late afternoon, so I used to drive her there, sit in the car marking my books from the Nurses' Training College, and then drive her home again. A young distant relative of ours called Laud Baddoo was also attending some classes, and he always made a point of having a nice chat with me when he was free. His friendliness and thoughtfulness quite restored my faith in the

Ghanaian personality! Winifred entered the medical school a year later in 1975, the only one, I think, with A-levels in both Mathematics and Biology, as well as Physics and Chemistry and the compulsory General Paper.

In 1974, Rosemary and also Ralph Mills-Tettey (our future son-in-law) completed their first degree in architecture. Rosemary went to England for three months and stayed with the Savages, while she worked with I.C. King and Partners, an architectural firm, which was very good experience for her.

When she arrived back, Rosemary and Ralph wanted to make their relationship clear, and therefore we had the traditional marriage ceremony on January 25th, 1975. The traditional marriage is in effect a marriage between two families. Although it is a binding commitment, people often referred to it as an 'engagement' ceremony. I can only assume that, years ago, the early missionaries would not approve of their new converts having a 'pagan' ceremony outside the Church. At the same time, the locals were determined to retain their ancient ceremonies, and so called it 'an engagement' to get round the difficulty. It is usually the women who keep the old customs going, adapting them as the years go by, and I admire them for it.

Some of my English friends wondered why Michael and I bothered with these customs. Why didn't we have a church wedding straight away? But I instinctively realized that the traditional marriage ceremony meant a lot to Michael's mother and sisters and the extended family. The groom's family sends a delegation of women to the bride's house with many gifts. Usually it is a foregone conclusion that their request for the girl in marriage will be accepted, but it is not completely unknown for the request to be rejected. In that case the couple would have a very difficult time if they went ahead and got married (or 'wedded') in church. Their union would never be accepted by the two families if the traditional ceremony had not been performed to their satisfaction.

While we were preparing for the ceremony, one 'busybody' in the family came to tell Michael that Rosemary and Ralph couldn't get married because they were too closely related! We were taken aback, and Michael rushed off to consult his mother who was a great authority on all traditional matters. After pausing for thought, she gave her verdict. It was true that one of Ralph's maternal ancestors was a sister to one of Rosemary's maternal ancestors. If it had been the case that one of Ralph's paternal ancestors and one of Rosemary's paternal ancestors had been brothers, the marriage would have been unacceptable. But, sisters on the maternal side - that was all right! I realized how much more complex Ghanaian 'rules' could be than British ones. We heaved a sigh of relief!

Later that year, Ayeley was born. About ten days before her birth, I heard that my mother had died. I felt sad, and guilty that I hadn't really been able to do my fair share of caring for her in her various illnesses - the burden had fallen on my older sister Doreen and my younger brother Peter - and I wasn't even able to attend the funeral. My other sister Jean had died at the early age of 42 from Hodgkin's disease. Once Ayeley arrived I was pretty busy and soon got over my grief. If there's something very special about one's first child, there is the same feeling of wonder about one's first grandchild. Of course, she had to be 'outdoored' and this took place at Ralph's father's house in Korle Gonno. The Mills-Tetteys are Gas, and our traditions are the same.

My mother in her younger days

There are seven clans of the Gas: Michael was from the Sempe clan, and the Mills-Tetteys from the Nketie Alata clan. We all helped to look after Ayeley while Rosemary worked through her two-year post-graduate course. Ralph by this time had already gone off to Ile-Ife in Nigeria as a lecturer at the University there. Things were really becoming difficult in Ghana economically, and lots of young professional Ghanaians went to greener pastures in Nigeria where they had oil to help their economy.

In September 1975 it was time for Jimmy to go off to boarding school - Mfantsipim, of course. He found it much easier to settle than Henry. This was partly due to the fact that bullying had been brought under control. And partly because the boys who had been in the lower forms when Henry was Dispensary Prefect (and treated so kindly by him) were now themselves in the Sixth Form, and treated Henry's young brother kindly. Perhaps this is one of the more attractive traits in the Ghanaian personality. A favour once received is never forgotten, and it will be returned, not always to the original benefactor, but to one of his relatives or friends, or even in the next generation!

We were quite happy to have the official church wedding for Rosemary and Ralph on September 25th 1976 when Ayeley was about a year old. Winifred was the maid of honour, and Jonathan Akai Nettey the best man. The service was held at the Ridge Church, with the reception at the Ridge Church School. Everything was done simply but nicely, and it was a very happy occasion. Jimmy was given charge of the cine-camera and made an excellent job of recording the occasion.

Back to Accra

Now that Jimmy was at Mfantsipim, and Karley still at Wesley Girls', we made many trips to Cape Coast to visit them both, and we often stayed with Michael's cousin Harry Acquaye-Baddoo and his wife Esther. It was a pleasant change from Accra.

I found the way the Gas named their children very interesting. It was more complicated than the day names used by many ethnic groups in Ghana. Each division had its own sets of names. To take Michael and Harry's families as an example: in one generation the first boy would be Allotey, the second boy Allotei, the third boy Addoquaye and so on. The first girl would be Adoley, the second Adorkor, the third Adokale and so one. In the next generation there would be different sets of names: the first boy would be Kpakpo, the second Akwei (or Acquaye) the third Addo, while the girls would be Aku, then Adukwei, then Kale. (We spelt our daughter's name 'Karley' so that the English relatives would pronounce it correctly). The following generation would go back to the first two sets of names, and so children are named after their grandfather's siblings. Of course the list is quite long - I have only mentioned the first few names of each set. Twins are considered to be a great blessing, and there are special names for them, as well as for the boy or girl born immediately after them.

So Esther and Harry's children had the same names as ours, except that they had four girls so the fourth was Mootso, and we had a second boy Akwei, but they had only one, Kpakpo. When I first arrived in the Gold Coast, and people were told our eldest daughter was called Aku, I couldn't understand why one person might exclaim, 'Oh, you are my grandmother!' and give her a big hug. Later everything became plain! Esther taught Art at Wesley Girls' High School, and Harry was on the staff at Mfantsipim, teaching English, and later Headmaster. He is also a fine local preacher in the Methodist Church. We really enjoyed our weekends with them and had a lot in common.

~ Chapter 13 ~

Michael Retires

In 1976, I went to England for a holiday by myself, and stayed with Ben and Margaret Tettey in Clapham, London. We had become friendly with the Tetteys seven years earlier in 1969 when Michael was transferred to Ho in the Volta Region. At that time, Ben was the Ghanaian chaplain at Mawuli School and Margaret was an English VSO (Voluntary Service Overseas) teacher at the same school. They met and fell in love, and we were invited to their wedding as we were the only 'mixed marriage' couple in Ho at the time. Margaret's parents came out for the wedding, and her father, who was an Anglican priest, helped conduct the service (even though he had been bitten by a snake a few days earlier!).

Now, in 1976, Ben was the Presbyterian/URC chaplain for the Ghanaian students in England. It was interesting hearing all about Ben's many projects as chaplain, and strangely enough, just round the corner, was the place where my father had lived with his first wife, Charlotte, in the flat over the butcher's shop where he worked. To my surprise, it was still a butcher's shop!

Ben felt he had a responsibility for all Ghanaian students, not just the church-going ones. He therefore worked closely with the University of London, and helped to explain to the welfare officers the special needs and thought processes of Ghanaian, and other African, students.

Michael, Henry, Ben Tettey and I

He also set up the Ghana Union, hoping that this would unite the efforts of Ghanaians from all the ethnic groups living in the

UK. Some of them still thought of themselves as Ashantis, Ewes, Gas, Fantis and so on, rather than as Ghanaians.

Subsequently he formed the Anglo-Ghanaian Society, linking British people who had worked in the Gold Coast and Ghana with Ghanaians living in the UK. As a result he became very friendly with Lord Listowel (the last Governor-General of the Gold Coast), and was often in and out of the House of Lords.

On my return to Ghana, I decided to have a change from teaching in the classroom. In fact, my hearing problem had worsened, and I could hardly hear what the students said, especially as they spoke more softly when they wanted to be respectful. I had seen an advertisement for someone to work at the Institute of Adult Education at the University of Ghana, Legon. I applied, was interviewed, and got the job. I was to work in the Correspondence Course Unit, writing lessons for the English Language O-level course. The students would then not have to buy text books which were difficult to obtain at that time.

I enjoyed the challenge, and the Editorial Board meetings. Sometimes we went for a weekend to the Sekondi-Takoradi Workers' College where we read over drafts of the lessons for several subjects. The other members of the Board were in the habit of tearing one's carefully written lesson to shreds. This was very painful at first, but one got used to it, and the rewritten lessons were all the better for the criticism. I shared an office with Mr Djokoto who was writing the Maths lessons.

Staff at the Institute of Adult Education, Legon

Henry went to England again in 1977, when he was a medical student, staying with the Saunders who lived in Stevenage to do an elective in anaesthetics at the Queen Elizabeth II Hospital in Welwyn Garden City, where Betty also worked as a social worker with psychiatric patients. He gained a lot from this experience, and we as a family were becoming closer to the Saunders family, after many years of simply keeping in touch with Christmas cards and occasional letters. Henry enjoyed the way Chris, like his dad Alan, was very practically minded with regard to technical things, and was always 'fixing' things that went wrong. This was not so common in Ghana (again, things may have changed), where the more educated people would call in others like carpenters, plumbers and masons to deal with quite everyday problems. Henry learnt a lot about keeping a car in good running order, and

Michael Retires

put this to good use when he got his own car.

Meanwhile Michael had retired in 1976 as Director of Medical Services. He was only fifty-five, but the retiring age had been fixed when the expatriates were around and had never been changed, possibly to make unemployment seem lower. He was asked to stay on for an extra six months, while they looked for someone to replace him. I remember that he was given a farewell banquet at State House and presented with a silver tray! On retirement, most Ghanaians quickly found another job, or continued 'on contract' for another five or even ten years. I was surprised that Michael, usually so full of energy, didn't seem very enthusiastic about getting another job. He tried various things - mostly in private clinics as he was still interested in clinical medicine - but nothing seemed to work out.

It seemed as though he would happily have stopped working altogether, but pensions were rapidly losing their value with inflation. The Acheampong regime, after starting out quite well, was beset by the usual problems of inefficiency and corruption, and life was very hard for most people. I was not earning much, as I was on a Ghanaian and not an expatriate contract. The children were still at various stages of their education - Rosemary married, with a child, but still completing her professional exam, Henry and Winifred at medical school, Karley and Jimmy still at school.

Of course, on his retirement, we had to move out of government accommodation, and by this time we had a second house at South Odorkor. The house was in a large estate built by the government, and as Michael owned a piece of the land they had to acquire compulsorily, he was not only given compensation, but also allowed to buy one of the houses being built.

Most Ghanaian men feel they have fulfilled their responsibilities when they have, first of all, paid for their children's education, and secondly, built a house or even more than one, and thirdly, given their parents good funerals. Michael had certainly done well fulfilling these three responsibilities. Soon after his retirement, his mother died, and he organized a fitting wake keeping (at the Lartebiokorshie house) and funeral service at Wesley.

In 1978, we had an interesting visitor for six months - Mark Saunders, the youngest son of Betty and Alan, whom we were gradually becoming closer to. Eighteen-year-old Mark had passed his A-levels and was taking a 'gap' year before going to Bristol University. We greatly enjoyed having him, although I often wished he had come with a friend, so that the two of them could go off together occasionally, exploring the town. We helped him get a job teaching at the Accra Academy. As he had just got good results, he found it quite manageable teaching A-level Physics - even though some of the students were older than himself.

He seemed to enjoy Ghanaian food, too, which pleased our cook, an older relative who came in daily. She declared he was 'putting on weight', and this in Ghana is always considered to be a

Alan and Betty Saunders

great compliment to the person addressed, and to the person cooking for him! We hoped Mark was not finding the evenings too boring. Fortunately, he had brought plenty of books to read. Later when Henry had qualified, and Mark was also on holiday, they set off to the north together. They journeyed on long-distance state transport, and stayed with relatives in Kumasi and Tamale, one being Dr Acquaye, now Professor of Haematology.

Every morning we dropped Mark off at the Accra Academy (see map on page 184) before Michael and I went on to our respective jobs. Mark was thrown in at the deep end and had to make his own way home every afternoon. On one occasion when for some reason I was at home, there was suddenly a terrible storm - rain pelting down enough to cause flooding, lightning flashes, claps of thunder, and strong winds almost like a tornado - just at the time when Mark and Michael would be making their way home. I was alarmed, and felt that some tragedy was bound to befall one or another of them - or both.

I vividly imagined how dreadful it would be if I had to get in touch with Mark's parents to give them bad news. However I set about cleaning all the windows, upstairs and downstairs, to push such thoughts out of my mind. Those of you who are familiar with louvred windows fitted with glass blades know how one has to concentrate in order to avoid cutting oneself on the occasional blade not always expertly finished off. Those windows have never had such a wonderful clean either before or since! Eventually Mark appeared, safe and sound, but looking like a drowned rat. He had to shelter under some empty tables suddenly abandoned in a mini-market. Then Michael returned in the car, which had not been swept away in the floods after all, and I breathed again.

Later that year Lily died, and I felt the loss keenly. She had been the one to write so regularly giving me news of the rest of the family. I was still working at Legon, and every lunchtime I drove to the top of the hill where the Vice-Chancellor's residence is, parked the car under the trees, ate my sandwiches, and had a quiet weep. Again I was not able to attend the funeral.

Michael Retires

Lily

The following year, Ray Dudding, the husband of my old friend Joyce, died after a short illness. This was a great shock for her and her two daughters Janet and Sheila, and I was sorry I wasn't nearer to give some support. In fact I was slowly losing touch with friends and family in England. As things became more and more difficult in Ghana, I appreciated those who kept up with me, even though I had no energy to keep up with them. One hardly liked to admit that the country one had such high hopes for was not living up to expectations. We had already had four coups in twelve years and the economy was in a mess.

At this time Michael was not happily settled in any permanent job. He might have enjoyed being back at Headquarters, not as Director, but working on the Public Health Act. He had always been keen on this being passed, and the lack of it was one of his disappointments as Director. This idea seemed unlikely to happen, as nobody wanted a former Director back at Headquarters!

However, in 1978, after Mark had gone back home, Michael was asked by the World Health Organisation to go to the Gambia and Liberia to write a report on their health services and possible developments in the future. The letter asking him to do this was sent to the Ministry of Health, and he very nearly did not receive it. Was someone deliberately blocking his getting it, or am I being cynical again?

He went, made a good job of his assignment, and earned enough money to pay off the mortgage on the South Odorkor House. Possibly, we thought, he would be asked to undertake more trips for the WHO and our financial problems would be solved!

The months went by, and on the morning of June 4th, 1979, Michael and I woke up late, and didn't switch the radio on as we usually did. Michael wasn't working at that time and stayed at home, and I quickly got ready and set off for work at Legon. When we were living at City Corner it was a fairly short eight kilometres journey along Independence Avenue and Liberation Road to get to the main entrance of the University. After Michael's retirement and our move to South Odorkor, it was a much longer 24 kilometre journey. I could have gone right round the Ring Road and then up Liberation Road to the main entrance, but I preferred to turn off at the cemetery and go through Kaneshie, Tesano and Achimota (see map on page 184). There was less traffic and it was more interesting, with each suburb having its own 'character'. I then entered the University campus by the back entrance instead of by the main gate.

Michael and I attended Wesley Church where he was choirmaster/organist. I still found the service very formal compared with Methodist services in England. There were a lot of set prayers, responses and we regularly sang the Te Deum and two other chants every week. I tried to adapt and, as part of my strategy to get to know and enjoy the set prayers, I fell into the habit of silently reciting the General Thanksgiving as I went along to work. Of course, this would normally take only a few minutes, but my thoughts often wandered, and this exercise kept me occupied for quite a bit of the half-hour journey. I was also very bad at learning things by heart, and often had to start again at the beginning! Here is a fairly typical example of what went through my head -

' "Almighty God, Father of all Mercies" - is that right, or should it be "Almighty and most Merciful Father"? No, that's the General Confession! Let me start again "Almighty God, Father of All Mercies, we Thine unworthy servants" - Well, I don't think I'm all that unworthy, I do my best! And why servants when we have just called him Father? Surely children would be more appropriate, or friends, partners, even lovers? What about Tillich's "ground of being"?.... I wonder how Rosemary is in Ile-Ife? - it will soon be time for the baby to arrive! Now where was I?.... "we Thine unworthy servants do give Thee humble and hearty thanks".... I like the alliteration!.... "for all Thy goodness and loving kindness to us and to all men." '

Wesley Church

And so I rambled on! On the morning of June 4th my thoughts were a little different.... ' "We thank Thee for our creation, preservation, and all the blessings of this life" - I like that too. But I wonder why there don't seem to be any people about. Is it a public holiday? Where are all the children going to school? Very strange! There's usually a bit of traffic - "and for Thy inestimable love in the redemption of the world....." It really is strange. Everywhere seems to be deserted!'

Michael Retires

I don't think I ever got to the end of the General Thanksgiving that morning. As I approached Achimota, some soldiers flagged me down. There was nothing particularly unusual about this, as we were under military rule. I dutifully got out, opened the boot for their inspection, and answered questions about where I was going. Back in the driving seat, I waved and drove off. Still nobody about! I arrived at the Institute of Adult Education and the place was deserted. At last I saw an office worker who lived on campus.

Office Worker: However did you get here?

Me: Well, I came by car as usual, but there doesn't seem to be anyone about. What's going on?

Office Worker: Don't you know there's been a coup? There's fighting all over the place. Jerry Rawlings and his supporters are trying to overthrow the government!

Me: (I was speechless)

Apparently fighting had been going on since the early hours at Burma Camp, and both sides were trying to take over Broadcasting House and the Airport. No wonder everybody was staying at home and the streets were deserted. Because of the route I took, I had avoided all the trouble spots. I quickly made my way to Volta Hall, the Women's Hall where Karley was in residence as a student, in order to take her home. She absolutely refused to go with me. All the students strongly supported

To Ghana with Love

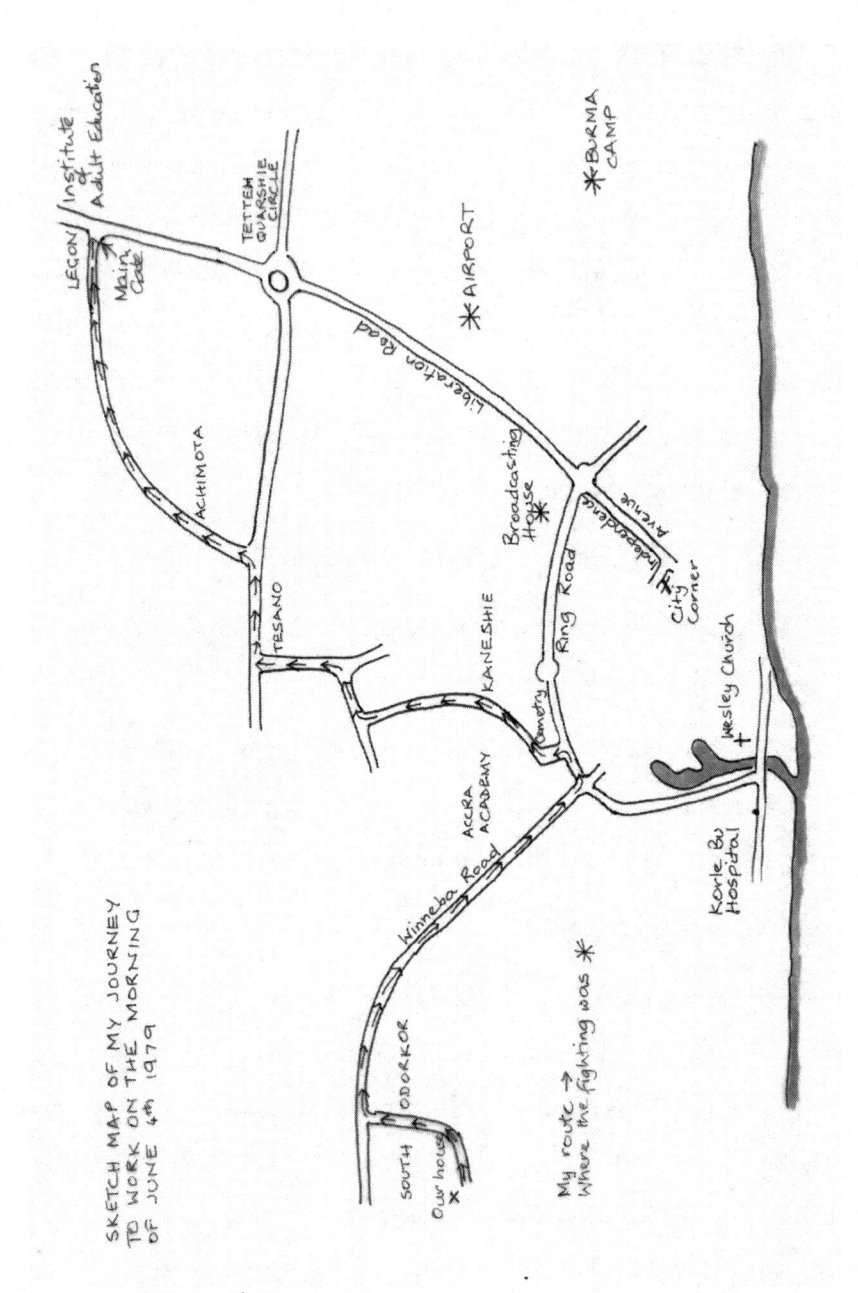

Journey to Work, 4th June 1979

184

Michael Retires

Rawlings, and had every confidence that, when the fighting was over, he would land at Legon in his helicopter and thank them for their support. This did happen, and Karley had a wonderful view of him being carried shoulder high by the men students!

I drove home, more fearfully this time, and Michael and I stayed in for three days listening to the radio. First Major-General Odartey-Wellington came on Radio Ghana to say the coup had failed. An hour or two later Jerry Rawlings announced the coup had succeeded. Often we had to tune in to the BBC World Service to find out what was really going on. Rawlings was indeed a very charismatic leader, and the masses cheered his emotional speeches about the need for accountability and honesty. The people had suffered too much in recent years. Ironically, because he was half Scottish and half Ghanaian, under normal circumstances, under the constitution, he would not qualify as Head of State.

A few days later, people were horrified when General (now Mr - he had been stripped of his army rank) Acheampong and General Utuka were executed by firing squad. A week later, six more of the overthrown government were also executed - General Akuffo, General Afrifa, Air Vice-Marshall Boakye, General Kotei, Rear-Admiral Amedume and Colonel Felli. This had never happened before in previous coups, which had been relatively peaceful. We were thankful that our personal friend General Ankrah was not touched.

A lot of corrupt people were brought to book, and to his credit, Rawlings carried out the elections that had been planned by the previous government. He handed over power to Hilla Limann and the People's National Party on September 24th, 1979, barely four months after the coup. The occasion was full of pomp and ceremony, and emotionally charged. The whole country felt proud that this young, impulsive and charismatic 'rebel' had not blocked the transition back to democracy. Not many military rulers have done that after such a short period.

~ Chapter 14 ~

The Younger Generation Leave Home

In the late 1970's, we decided to move to our house in Lartebiokorshie. Michael had given his sister Victoria and her husband Victor a quarter of the land at Lartebiokorshie, on which to build a house for themselves. They had occupied our house while it was being built, and now their house was ready for them to move in. By living in Winchmore House (as we called it) at Lartebiokorshie, we could find tenants for the South Odorkor House and use the rent for essentials. Things were still very difficult financially.

I was beginning to realise how 'cushioned' we had previously been, living in the government bungalows built for the Europeans in residential areas far removed from the noise and hurly-burly in the centre of the town. There, rubbish had been collected daily, and we had plenty of help with gardening, guarding the house at night, and speedy assistance when lights failed or water stopped running or a snake got into the outside kitchen. Now we were closer to the ordinary people and living at the grass-roots level. If the car broke down or there were no spare parts available, we could no longer call for an office car and driver, but had to rely on a dilapidated taxi or an overcrowded bus - or lifts from friends.

On the positive side, it was nice to see more of Victoria and Victor as neighbours, and also Michael's sister, Marian and her husband, Robert, who also lived nearby. Their children sometimes came to spend Saturdays with us, and I helped them learn to play the piano. Robert was a real tower of strength, and was able to help us out on many occasions as he was the only close relative with a car. He kept this in immaculate order, and his help, always given quietly without fuss, was much appreciated for "engagement" ceremonies and weddings.

Henry had done well with a prize in Medicine and a Distinction in Pharmacology, and after his housemanship went off to England hoping to specialize in anaesthesia. At that time, Doreen and Tom were having a tough time looking after Doreen's mother, who was always very frail, and her father who was seriously ill. Henry arrived just in time to help them out while he was waiting to take his Professional and Linguistic Assessment Board (PLAB) exam. A pass was needed before he was allowed to practise medicine in England. As Doreen said, it was an answer to their prayers. Soon afterwards, her parents moved to Ashley Lodge Nursing Home not too far from their home in Lymington in Hampshire.

Henry again stayed with the Saunders, while he was waiting to satisfy the requirements before getting a medical job. He worked in a bakery for six weeks to earn a bit of money, using Marion's bicycle to get there. He was not the only visitor as Martin and Phil Bishop were also staying there. Henry remembers the lively discussions they had sitting round the table, after a gorgeous Sunday roast. The subjects ranged from philosophy to engineering, from politics to evolution. These Sunday discussions have become a great tradition in the Saunders household.

Rosemary had by this time joined Ralph in Ile-Ife in Nigeria, and had her second daughter, Ayorkor. Karley was nearing the end of her degree course at the University of Ghana, Legon, and Jimmy was at Mfantsipim. So it was only Winifred who was around as a medical student at Korle Bu to give me support when Michael was diagnosed with cancer of the large bowel. Professor Archampong operated very successfully. He told me privately that the prognosis was not very good, and he wished it had been diagnosed much earlier. I appreciated his being frank with me, and prepared myself for any eventuality. I now realized why Michael had lost his usual energy on his retirement, and wondered how he had coped so well with the WHO assignment. As it was, thanks to Professor Archampong's good work, he lived for seventeen years after the operation.

At this critical time, Michael's salary failed to turn up (due to confusion or perhaps even corruption), and inflation was running at 200 per cent. Now we really were in need - desperate need - and yet we managed somehow. Friends and relatives in England helped in a very practical, understanding way. Help also came from Ghanaian relatives whom we had previously helped, and from some we had never helped. Times were tough for all of us, but the help was given graciously and without fuss. The relationship between myself and my Ghanaian relatives underwent a subtle change for the better, although it had always been quite good. They were far better able to cope and survive in the difficult conditions in which we all found ourselves. I was needing and receiving help instead of giving it, and it was a salutary experience.

In 1980, the mother of Rachel (Henry's future wife) died in Edinburgh. Leonora Evans-Anfom was a remarkable African-American lady whom everyone loved and admired. Her body was flown to Accra, where she was to be buried, and everyone, including Michael and myself, flocked to her wake-keeping and funeral to show the great affection and esteem in which she was held. Rachel was in her final year as a law student, and bravely carried on.

In the summer of 1980, it happened that all our children (grown-ups, really!) were in England! Henry was already there as a qualified doctor, and Winifred was doing an elective at

Sir Geoffrey Keynes and Jim

St Bartholomew's Hospital where Michael had once been a medical student. Rosemary and Ralph had decided to go from Nigeria on a visit to England taking Ayeley with them. They passed through Accra to leave Ayorkor with us, as she was far too young to enjoy a trip abroad. Karley, having graduated, was going as a reward for all her hard work, and it happened that her friend Kwesi, later her husband, was also there visiting his father in Bedford.

Finally Jimmy was there on a more permanent basis. Having got good results in his O-levels at Mfantsipim, he had been invited by the Saunders to stay with them for two years to do his sixth form course at Alleynes School in Stevenage, where their boys had been educated. Of course his brother and sisters all visited him at the Saunders, and it was Karley who noticed how well organised Betty was as a mother with a career. She admired her well-stocked freezer, and how Betty produced wonderful meals for large numbers of people without any fuss. I'm sure that she decided to emulate her in the years that lay ahead! Her only problem was calling her 'Betty' which she found rather improper for someone old enough to be her mother. But Betty insisted upon it!

As for Jimmy, he quickly became Jim, and Betty and Alan took seriously the job of explaining all sorts of aspects of British culture, history and food. They really helped him settle down, and integrate into the British way of life. They realised that little things mattered, and gently corrected his tendency to refer to 'Mummy and Daddy', replacing it with 'Mum and Dad', and to give up using the incorrect (but common) Ghanaian pronunciation 'arx' and replace it with the correct 'ask'.

Michael and I felt strange without them all, but I got to know my second little granddaughter very well, and the Armah daughters, Solace and Martha next door, gave me a helping hand looking after her. The younger generation had a wonderful time meeting up with all those in London - Ken and Ella and family, the Savages, and Lily's friend Mabel - as well as the Saunders in Stevenage, and the Pages in Carbrooke. They enjoyed all the luxuries in the affluent world after experiencing the tough times in Ghana - although Nigeria was not so bad at that time.

The Younger Generation Leave Home

Soon Rosemary and Ralph (having picked up Ayorkor on the way) were back in Ile-Ife, and Winifred back at Korle Bu, soon to qualify as the second doctor in the family. Karley was back and had promised to go with three other graduates to Jirapa in the far north, for her National Service. Somehow the other three dropped out, and Karley did not like the idea of travelling such a long way and being there by herself. She therefore went to Cape Coast and asked Miss Garnett if she could do her National Service at Wesley Girls' High School instead. Karley was called Margaret at school, and the following conversation ensued:

Miss G.: But I thought you were going to Jirapa, Margaret?

Karley: Yes, Miss Garnett, but ...

Miss G.: Did you not promise to go, Margaret?

Karley: Yes, Miss Garnett, but ...

Miss G.: Then you must go! Your services are needed much more in the north than here at Wesley Girls'!

So Karley dared not disobey Miss Garnett, and did go, travelling by herself, and having all sorts of adventures on the way. She travelled by State Transport, which often, in those difficult days, broke down or was delayed for various reasons. Once they missed the ferry and had to sleep by the river before proceeding the next day. There was always a group of Ga women, who took it upon themselves to look after and chaperone her when there were long delays. As the post was so unreliable from the far north, we did not hear about her adventures until she came home at the end of each term! She enjoyed the experience and met some interesting volunteers from abroad. They hired bicycles and explored the area, even going over the border to the Upper Volta, which was later renamed Burkina Faso. She persuaded Kwesi to visit her and share her experience of life in the north, which is so different in many ways from the south.

It was in the late 1970's, that I noticed another 'obroni' (white person) sitting, dressed very smartly, in the 99.9% black Wesley Church congregation every Sunday. This was Joyce Engmann, whose husband was a Member of Parliament in Limann's government. Victor and Joyce had both lectured at Cape Coast University. As an MP, he needed to be in Accra and Joyce transferred to the University of Ghana, Legon, and they lived on campus with their three delightful daughters, Catherine, Dorothy and Mary. I often dropped in after work, and enjoyed getting Dorothy started on learning to play the piano. Joyce sometimes came to lunch at Winchmore House after the Sunday service at Wesley. In these difficult days, when so many Europeans - and Ghanaians too - had left Ghana, it was a joy to have a friend who could understand how one longed for Ghana to do well and achieve the potential she so obviously had.

On December 31st, 1981, I was at the New Year School at Legon. We had had an interesting lecture given by the President, Dr Hilla Limann, and formed a favourable impression of the new

The Younger Generation Leave Home

Head of State. He came over as intelligent, able, ready to listen, and not at all 'arrogant' (to Ghanaians this is the most heinous sin). Then a day or two later another coup! We could hardly believe it. It was fairly peaceful this time. Apparently Rawlings was not satisfied with the way things were going, and it was true that the economy was no better and corruption was rearing its ugly head again. Limann was being let down by his fellow politicians whom he could not control. A familiar story!

Immediately Limann was overthrown, all his cabinet and Members of Parliament had to report at the nearest police station, and Victor was sent to Nsawam Prison. Mercifully, he was released five weeks later, and Joyce went home after her lectures surprised and overjoyed to find him in the sitting-room surrounded by the children dancing with delight! Those five weeks were the longest in Joyce's life!

The first year of Rawlings PNDC (Provisional National Defence Council) government was extremely hard for everyone. The harvest failed because of poor rainfall. Added to this, Rawlings had allied himself with Gaddafi of Libya and Fidel Castro of Cuba, and the whole of the western democratic world was against him. They made life as difficult as possible for us. Petrol was sometimes unobtainable and people had to walk long distances to work. Food was short and the shelves in the shops empty. We couldn't even get red pens to mark our scripts! If it hadn't been for my sisters-in-law, who always knew where to get the local food, like kenkey, we would hardly have survived.

Sometimes we ate kokonte, considered to be the poor man's diet. If the flour was not properly prepared (from cassava), it could be dangerous. From time to time there would be a headline in the newspaper - 'FAMILY OF SIX DIE AFTER MEAL OF KOKONTE'. Our dear elderly cook knew the best market woman to buy the flour from and we never suffered any ill effects. She would remind me of this if I complained of any of her shortcomings - which were very few actually. I also remember one patient (probably a relative) who used to come to the house to consult Michael. She was a baker, and whenever she had supplies of flour she would bring us a few loaves of bread. My eyes used to light up! I can honestly say it was the first time in my life that I experienced what it was like to feel really hungry. At the same time, the atmosphere was similar to wartime Britain in the early 1940's. We all helped each other, and there was a feeling of unity and determination. However, a lot of professionals left the country, and the universities were definitely short staffed, and lacking books and equipment.

We were pleased therefore that Jim was doing so well in England. Having passed his A-levels, he was offered a place at Trinity College in Cambridge. As Michael said later at Jim and Nancy's wedding 'the shy schoolboy Jimmy had matured into the resolute young man Jim!' While waiting to go up to Cambridge University, he worked at Luton, staying at the home of a friend of the Saunders family, Joan Samuel, who was the widow of a mixed race marriage and lived with her elderly mother. He concentrated in his after-work hours on studying for his French O-level, successfully completing the course in 6 months. His school had belatedly realised that he needed an O-level in a foreign language in order to enter Cambridge.

Meanwhile, Betty and Alan continued to provide a base for him in Stevenage for five more years until he graduated and worked for a year. They had quietly strengthened his capabilities as an engineer, encouraging him to be precise rather than vague, and practical as well as academic. They had also helped him through the various stages all immigrants face – first of all culture shock, followed by understanding the new system, learning to live within it, and finally being able to have authority within the system. An added excitement living in their household was the fact that their daughter Marion, became the British high-board diving champion, and took part in the 1980 Olympics in Moscow!

The importance of life not being 'all work' was not forgotten. Soon after his arrival, they took him to London to celebrate his 18th birthday by seeing 'Oklahoma'. That was his first experience of a London theatre. Later he took up piano lessons again; he made some good friends and went on a cycling trip with one of them round the Cotswolds - Henry had made sure that he had a good bicycle.

Marion at 'Service to Sport' award

In November, 1982, Rosemary decided to go to England to have her third child. Henry rented a flat in Sheffield, and shared it with Rosemary and Winifred who was also there at the time. How nice to think that the siblings were keeping in touch and helping each other. How nice, too, that they all have a great affection for England as well as Ghana. Rosemary had her third daughter, Ayikai Charlotte, at Jessops Hospital, which was going to be the chosen place for the arrival of five of our grandchildren.

In Ghana life did go on, though we all got noticeably thinner - even the notoriously overweight market women! Michael and I made a few trips to stay with Rosemary and Ralph still working at

The Younger Generation Leave Home

the University of Ile-Ife, Nigeria, where things were not so tough. On one of these visits, Michael was suddenly musically inspired in the middle of the night! He leapt out of bed, and jotted down (in tonic sol-fa, of course) the tune for a Christmas melody. The next day, he worked hard composing a three-part Christmas round in Ga, called "Herode Kpokpo". This round was sung by the Wesley Church choir that Christmas, and subsequently became very popular in Accra. Even now, it can be heard in various churches at Christmas time. The general meaning (with lots of repetition) is "Herod trembled and was frightened and the whole of Jerusalem with him". Perhaps with so many military coups and changes of government, people were amused at the idea of those in power trembling and being frightened!

Back in Ghana, on 23rd July 1983, we had Karley and Kwesi's traditional marriage ceremony followed by their church wedding on 12th April 1984. Rosemary had three daughters now, but she was able to come from Nigeria to help organize it all, again at the Ridge Church. She stayed to help with Henry and Rachel's traditional wedding ceremony on 28th April, and was part of the delegation bearing gifts to her future sister-in-law's family. Of course this was at Rachel's father's house, Leonora Lodge. Rachel was there but not Henry! This sounds strange I know to English ears, but that didn't prevent it from being valid and binding. It is the two families that are important on such an occasion, not the individuals!

By 1984, I was due to retire and I suggested to Michael that it would be a good idea for us to go to England for a longer stay. Henry had bought a small house in Dronfield (near Sheffield) and with his usual generosity said we could use it. I really felt I needed a break from all the hardships in Ghana at that time. Jerry Rawlings did eventually bring about economic growth, but it didn't happen over night.

Winifred had qualified and completed her housemanship, and had also gone off to England. She was determined to specialise in paediatrics, although she had been warned that it was a difficult discipline for those from abroad to get into. She passed the Professional and Linguistic Assessment Board (PLAB) exam, and did a couple of clinical attachments in hospitals in Sheffield and a medical house job in Stockport. She was then called for her first interview for a paediatric job on the Isle of Wight, and got the appointment. So much for the pessimists!

While we were planning to go to England, I realised that the only one left in Ghana would be Karley. As a child, she had always been rather overshadowed by her older sisters and brother. But after university, she turned out to be a very strong character and very good at her job as a Maths teacher. Maybe her marriage to Kwesi had something to do with that. They were both teaching at Wesley Girls' High School, and Karley was expecting their first child. Later she became Assistant Headmistress.

I did not like leaving her, and made up my mind to visit them in Cape Coast, so that I could visualize them in their new accommodation. We didn't have enough petrol to go by car, so I had to go by State Transport. I had to be at the station at 5 am in order to be sure of getting a ticket. After that I had to wait patiently until noon before I got on the long-distance bus. Kwesi was waiting for me at the Cape Coast station when I arrived at 2 pm totally exhausted. We got a taxi and went to their new home. I was pleased I had made the effort, and we had a nice weekend. On Monday I was supposed to be getting a lift in the school bus, which was going to Accra that day. Somehow I missed it and saw it flashing past their block of flats! So I had another wearisome journey on the State Transport bus to get home.

Back in Accra, we had to get the money together to buy our tickets to England. On retirement I was given a gratuity, not a pension. It was not worth much as I had not worked for very many years, and in any case inflation had made such amounts pretty worthless. We had some sterling in our English bank account, and for the second time in our lives we decided to break the law! We changed an English cheque on the black market! The relative I did it through, laughed and said, 'Oh, so even you are dabbling in the black market now, are you? I am surprised!' I felt ashamed that I had ever had a 'holier than thou' attitude. Yes, it's easy to have high principles when one is well-off, but not so easy sticking to them when the going gets tough!

I was given a huge amount of Ghanaian notes in a large plastic bag, which I hid in the wardrobe. When I went to the Ghana Airways office to buy the tickets the next morning, I fully expected a heavy hand to come down on my shoulder any minute as I was marched away to the police station. But of course nothing happened because everyone was doing the same thing! Later the Forex Bureaux were set up and changing foreign money to cedis and vice versa was made legal. How sensible!

So we arrived in England and stayed at Stevenage before going up to Dronfield. It was a delight to see Jim, Winifred and Henry again. Henry and Winifred were following their chosen careers as doctors. We felt it was their own choice and that they hadn't been pushed into it just because their father was a doctor. Jim was reading Engineering at Trinity College, Cambridge and doing very

Jim's graduation in 1986

The Younger Generation Leave Home

well. We were grateful to the Saunders for having him to stay for seven years instead of the original two! At Cambridge, Jim met an English girl Nancy Price (later his wife) who was also reading Engineering and doing equally well. They both achieved first class degrees.

~ *Chapter 15* ~

Dronfield Days

I n 1984, we settled down nicely in Dronfield, which is in Derbyshire, halfway between Chesterfield (with its crooked spire) and Sheffield. The well-stocked shops were a few yards from Henry's house, and what a relief it was to be able to buy anything we needed, and never to feel hungry, after the tough times in Ghana. The ecumenical Methodist/Anglican/United Reformed Church (St Andrews), where we felt very much at home, was only a walking distance away. Dronfield must be one of the friendliest little towns in England, small enough to have a strong community spirit, and yet large enough to have a Sports Centre (with swimming pool) as well as amateur light opera and drama groups putting on musicals and plays at regular intervals in the large Civic Hall.

Michael quickly joined the church music group, and I went to the women's Monday afternoon fellowship, and we both made lasting friends. It was at St Andrew's Church that we discovered how good women ministers could be. Michael also found out about the Sheffield and District Organists' and Choirmasters' Association (SADOCA) and never missed a meeting. They organized day trips to churches with famous organs, and were a friendly crowd. Meanwhile I enrolled in classes for dressmaking and computers. Winifred had been living in Henry's house, and was well-known at the church, so at first we were simply 'Winifred's Mum and Dad'. When she moved on to her first paediatric job in the Isle of Wight, we gradually acquired our own identity and became 'Barbara and Michael'.

We were in Dronfield for ten years, and mostly it was a very happy period of our lives. Typically though, we still kept on the move, first of all living in Henry's house in Southcote Drive, then in Winifred's in Coniston Road, before finally settling in our own flat in sheltered accommodation at Hallowes Court in Cemetery Road (why such a dreary name - couldn't it have been named after a well-known Dronfieldian?). During those ten years, there were three marriages in the family, and nine of our grandchildren were born - not all in England, of course, but also in Ghana and Nigeria. Quite a record!

Michael playing an organ in Sheffield

The marriages first! In 1984, soon after our arrival, Henry and Rachel were planning to get married at Finchley Methodist Church in North London. This was arranged with the help of my cousin Dennis, and his warm-hearted wife, Winifred. I had stayed with Dennis' parents as a student, and Uncle Fred had 'given me away' at my wedding. Rosemary had stayed with them while doing her electives in London, and it was simply wonderful to be in close contact with them again. The service, on June 30th, was conducted by Rev Denis Creamer, an old school friend from my Winchmore Hill days. Another memorable occasion! Dr Adzo Apaloo, Rachel's friend from Aburi Girls' Secondary School was the bridesmaid, and Jim the best man. He made a very good speech, and maybe the fact that the 'baby' of the family was now an adult finally sank in!

A few years later, in 1987, when we were living with our daughter Winifred and she was working at Rotherham near Sheffield, Samuel Ohene (her future husband) had just come to Cardiff in Wales to complete his Captain's certificate. He had originally trained at the Ghana Nautical College (now Regional Maritime University, Accra). When he and his friends were nearing the end of their training, the Ghana government sold off all the Black Star Line ships, and so they had to find jobs abroad. He had been navigating ships for some time, in the Far East. He and Winifred knew each other because they had both been at Achimota together, and sat in the same classroom as young teenagers. Samuel got in touch with Winifred, and the rest is history! He was once asked how he had tracked Winifred down in the small town of Dronfield, and he replied, 'I used my navigational instincts!'

We arranged to have their traditional marriage in Ghana on August 20th, 1988. Samuel had gone off navigating an Ethiopian Line ship called 'Nebelbal' (the name means 'Fire'!) in the Red Sea, and Winifred was still working at Rotherham. So neither of them would be at the traditional marriage ceremony, and nor would we. Even stranger to English ears! But it was still valid and binding with Michael's sisters representing our family, and Samuel's mother, sister and uncle representing his. We had a video recording of the ceremony, and in Dronfield we all went for a celebratory lunch at the local pub on that day.

Less than a month later, on September 10th, Jim and Nancy, who had met in Cambridge, were married at the Baptist Church in Cheam, where Nancy's parents live. Nancy's mother is a wonderful organizer, and after the service with family, friends and congregation present, the reception was held in a marquee in the Prices' garden. It was beautifully decorated in pink and white, and the meal was superb, even the fruit dessert echoed the colours of the Ghana flag - red strawberries, yellow star fruit, and green kiwis. All the speeches were entertaining and amusing - Paul's, Jim's, Michael's and best man Matthew's. Afterwards Jim and Nancy went off on their honeymoon on the Greek island of Samos.

Now all our five children are married, and our 'in-laws' are a varied lot - four are Ghanaian but from different ethnic groups - two Gas, one Fante, one Akwapim/Ashanti - and one is English. What could be better? They also comprise one architect, one lawyer, one master mariner, one graduate teacher and one civil engineer. What more could we ask, as parents? We hope the in-laws are equally pleased. As I write, they are all still happily married. They have all gone their separate ways, and made their own choices. In spite of having very different views on politics, religion, Ghanaian culture and so on, they have remained close, and supported each other especially when difficulties crop up.

So much for the marriages! Now for the grandchildren. Soon after Henry and Rachel's wedding, Karley came to England to have her first child. There was a serious shortage of drugs in Ghana (as well as of everything else) and we thought Karley should be with us in England for this event. The Ghanaian tradition also demands that an expectant woman should go back to her mother to have her first child. Our first grandson, Kweku, was born in September 1984 at Jessops Hospital in Sheffield.

Karley stayed with us for six months because then anything she took back - and they needed a lot of essentials - would be tax-free. How I enjoyed bathing Kweku every morning and evening! The community midwife, Sister Desborough, was so helpful and became a staunch friend of the whole family. She even found a pram we could borrow for Karley's fairly brief stay. Of course Karley missed Kwesi but the long letters he sent kept her going - she would tuck the latest one into her dressing-gown pocket and take it out at intervals to reread it. At Christmas, the church carol singers came and sang 'Away in a manger' on our doorstep especially for Claud (his other name, after his paternal grandfather).

Six months after Karley and baby Kweku went back to Ghana, Henry and Rachel's first child, Leonora, was born in Poole where Henry was working. We were able to stay there for a while and give a helping hand. This is always satisfying especially when one does not have full responsibility, and this is one of the perks of

Kweku, Ato, Karley and Kwesi - 1991

being a grandparent. By this time, Doreen and Tom had moved from Norfolk to Doreen's parents' house in Lymington. We were pleased when Leonora was baptised at the Lymington Methodist Church.

After that, Rosemary and her three girls arrived from Nigeria for an academic year. Never a dull moment! Ralph had a sabbatical and was spending it in Holland. A few months before their arrival, we had received a letter from Rosemary, saying that she had joined the Baha'i faith. This was a bolt from the blue, as we had never heard of this faith. We didn't quite know what to expect. We were soon reassured when Rosemary and the children arrived and quickly got in touch with other Baha'is living in Dronfield.

Amongst other things, they believe that the second coming of Christ has already taken place in the birth of Baha'u'llah, the founder of their faith. Certainly the character and life style of those Baha'is we met showed all the Christian 'fruits of the spirit', and the book I read called 'Thief in the Night' by William Sears had the ring of truth about it. I was willing to believe it was the right path for Rosemary, but I did not feel God was pushing (or even nudging) me to leave the Christian Church to join them. Everybody has their own spiritual journey to make.

Ralph, Ayeley, Yoki, Kai, Rosemary and Niiayitey - 1993

Dronfield Days

The house was really too small for three adults (four when Ralph visited) and three children, but it was worth it. Ayeley enjoyed being a first year secondary schoolgirl, and Yoki fitted in very well at St Andrew's Primary School (in the same building as the church). Her hero was Mr Lane, her class teacher, and every day we had to hear what he had said and done. One day Yoki went up to Mr Lane's desk to have her sums marked. When he finished he frowned and said, 'This is terrible!!!!!!... (pause).... All right again!' Then he gave her an encouraging smile. She thought this exceedingly funny.

I got to know Kai well as she was at home all day except for a couple of hours at playgroup each weekday. Maybe I could have done better! Whenever I was going to make a cake, she would say, 'Can I help you. Grandma?' and I would reply, 'Well, not this time, dear, because it's just a quick cake.' At last, one day she said, 'Grandma, can we make a slow cake today?'

Rosemary and the girls went back to Nigeria and it didn't seem long before Leonora's little sister, Shevon, was born in Ballymoney in Northern Ireland. I went there by air to give a hand, once again enjoying my role of grandmother helping by day but not having any sleepless nights. Later that year, Karley and Kwesi had their second son, Ato, in Ghana. He was also named 'Michael' after his maternal grandfather.

Many Ghanaians in England settle in big cities like London and Birmingham where their social life revolves round their fellow

Ghanaians. We felt we had the best of both worlds with plenty of English friends, but without losing touch with Ghana, through our many visitors and also Ghanaians living nearby. Our old friends Joan and Silas Dodu had a house in Sheffield, and we often visited them and their daughters too, three of whom eventually settled in Dronfield. Sadly Joan lost her battle with cancer in 1988, and we greatly miss her. Joyce Engmann also came and settled in Jordanthorpe and Katherine (nee Phillips) and Philip Gardiner in Barlborough - both on the outskirts of Sheffield. We also had visitors from London - the Saakwa-Mantes and the Tetteys.

Myself and Nora

There is no point in going to another country and mixing only with one's own compatriots, but everybody does it. Many of the British in the old Gold Coast hardly went into the homes of ordinary Gold Coasters, but had their round of cocktail parties and social activities with other expatriates. Hopefully things are changing, but many Ghanaians are also hardly going into the homes of ordinary British families. They are repeating the mistakes of expatriates everywhere.

In 1989 Winifred had Almaz, again at Jessops, and again visited by Sister Desborough. In 1991, Yolanda arrived. It was interesting being in Dronfield and watching these two little girls growing up over a period of years instead of just a few months or weeks here and there as with the other grandchildren. The grandchildren in Dronfield are, of course, 75% Ghanaian (with looks to match their inheritance), and Dronfield was, at that time, almost wholly 'white'. In such circumstances, the parents have to make a conscious effort to ensure that their children 'fit in' with their local environment. The Ohene children were encouraged to make lots of friends even when they were toddlers, and were in and out of each other's houses playing together and having 'sleepovers'. Their childhood has therefore been a very happy one. Perhaps later they may live and work elsewhere, but in childhood it is the 'here and now' that has to shape one's daily life.

It is even more important when children are 100% Ghanaian (or any other ethnic minority). Recently I was rather saddened to read the beautifully written book 'Black Gold of the Sun' by the accomplished writer Ekow Eshun. His parents obviously gave him all their care and love in his childhood, but one felt if only they

Winifred, Almaz, Samuel, Annabel and Yolanda - 2003

had gone the extra mile! If only they had had his English (and other non-Ghanaian) friends in and out of the house, and helped him make the most of the English culture and environment, a lot of the emotional trauma he went through might have been avoided.

Back to Dronfield! Michael was gaining quite a reputation for getting babies to sleep by putting them on his shoulder, which seemed to have some magical properties! Another year passed and, in 1992, Rosemary and Ralph had their son, Niiayitey, in Nigeria. This was quite a surprise, as it was nearly ten years after Kai was born. Six months later, Henry and Rachel had their third little girl, Ruth, in Accra. They had returned to Ghana in 1990, soon after Henry had passed both the FFARCS (now the FRCA - Fellow of the Royal College of Anaesthetists) and the FRCS (Fellow of the Royal College of Surgeons) - quite an achievement, and we were proud of him.

Henry, Leonora, Rachel, Ruth and Shevon - 1994

A year later, Jim and Nancy's first child was born. We were delighted to welcome their new-born son, Peter, as the girls in the family were seriously outnumbering the boys. His arrival completed the nine grandchildren born within our ten-year stay in Dronfield. We still had three more to come, making fifteen grandchildren altogether, eleven girls and four boys.

Kate, Peter, Harriet, Nancy and Jim - 1998

We started with three granddaughters, and also ended with three more granddaughters. Jim and Nancy's Kate was born in 1995 soon after we returned to Ghana in 1994. Winifred and Samuel's Annabel was born in 1997, and Jim and Nancy's Harriet in 1998. Sadly Michael did not live to see his two youngest granddaughters.

I wonder when I first had that weird feeling and thought, 'If it wasn't for me and my marriage to Michael, none of these individuals would be here!' It's a sobering thought. Looking to the future it is quite possible that by the end of the twenty-second century I might have a thousand descendents. But, by that time, my contribution to each one's genetic inheritance might be less than one per cent. What a mixture of self-importance and self-effacement we are bound to have! Not to mention the fact that one doesn't have to be a biological parent to have a great influence on children and future generations.

Another thought quickly follows, 'If my father's first wife had not died, or if he had not met my mother, I wouldn't be here either.' Looking back to my ancestors (as so many well-known people have done in the television series 'Who do you think you are?'), I realize that way back at the time of the Civil War in England, there must have been a thousand people marrying and begetting children who would eventually result in the birth of me. Do I ever give a thought, to their achievements and joys, as well as their struggles and disappointments?

~ *Chapter 16* ~

Back to Ghana to Face Bereavement

In 1990, we celebrated our Ruby Wedding anniversary. Our old and faithful friend, Doreen had suggested that we might celebrate it in Lymington, as this was a reasonably accessible venue for all those we hoped to invite. Three of our grown-up children were able to come - Henry, Winifred and Jim, and two daughters-in-law, Rachel and Nancy, as well as three of the eight grandchildren we then had. I was so pleased that my two brothers, Ken and Peter were able to come with their wives Ella and Jenny. Our old friends, the Saunders and the Tetteys, as well as, of course, the Pages completed the picture.

The adults all met at the lovely cliff-top hotel Westover Hall at Milford-on-Sea for lunch, later adjourning to Doreen and Tom's house where the children joined us for an informal get-together over tea. Here the highlight was the cake made by Winifred and decorated with five pink roses (one for each of our children), and eight rosebuds springing forth to represent our grandchildren at that time. It was a lovely sunny day, and we all enjoyed meeting together for such a happy occasion.

Ruby Wedding celebration

I have said that we were very happily settled in Dronfield, and this is true up to 1991. In this year, we went on a visit to Ghana. Looking back, I think I was the one who was more enthusiastic about going, and made all the arrangements. We enjoyed the trip very much, spending most of the time seeing relatives and old friends. We met up with Rosemary and Ralph who had come on a visit from Nigeria.

I returned to England leaving Michael to stay an extra fortnight. When he joined me two weeks later, I was surprised to

Back to Ghana to Face Bereavement

find that he was terribly worried about himself and aspects of his stay in England. I could see that these worries were quite unfounded. He who in his heyday had a reputation for his clinical acumen, seemed unable to diagnose himself, and see things in their proper perspective. The General Practitioner (family doctor) was very helpful, and from time to time Michael would get back to his normal cheerful self. Then his fears would resurface. I would sit down with him and would put forward all the reasons why his worries were unreasonable, and he would agree with every word I said. Yet a day or two later, his anxiety would be as strong as ever.

He was very homesick too and wanted to return to Ghana. However we carried on pretty normally for a year or two, with a few laughs over his imaginary problems, but I could see that for his own peace of mind it would be better if we returned to Accra. After all, I (or rather we) had enjoyed ten years in my own country (although Derbyshire was far from my home town of London!) and I was satisfied with that. Of course I did not look forward to yet another move, but after all I was used to it by this time. We were lucky to have a house to go back to.

So in 1994 we returned to Accra. Our house in South Odorkor had been occupied by a very unsatisfactory tenant and the house and garden were in a frightful state. Henry asked Rachel's cousin, Stella Evans-Anfom, to take on the mammoth task of putting everything to rights, and she made a wonderful job of it. On our return, Stella and her three daughters, Nana, Adjoa and Maame, lived downstairs and we lived upstairs. As the kitchen was downstairs, Stella prepared the main meals. We enjoyed their company, and admired the way Stella did not allow Nana's blindness to prevent her having a good education and a normal social life.

We enjoyed seeing more of Henry, who was at the Ghana Medical School at Korle Bu, and Karley, still working at Wesley Girls' High School in Cape Coast. Rosemary had already returned to Ghana ahead of Ralph, as they were going to leave Ile-Ife and resettle in Accra. Of course, we missed seeing Winifred and family several times a week, and Jim and family in Reading.

Unfortunately, soon after our return, Michael was diagnosed with cancer again. This was not something he had ever worried about! Everything possible was done, but this time the treatment was not successful, and he died two years after our return. I realised that some of his anxieties and fears, and his strong desire to return to his roots, were due to his undiagnosed illness. Perhaps he instinctively felt his life was drawing to its close, and he wanted to be in his own home town amongst his own people.

I felt very pleased that I had not argued, or insisted that he went back alone leaving me in Dronfield, which I could easily have done. I strongly believe that I have been guided concerning which path to take, at key moments in my life. Michael was happier even though he was ill, and even though some of his anxieties did not leave him. He had plenty of relatives and friends dropping in, and talking and praying with him. Henry was there to help the other consultants with treatment as he did not, in the end, wish to return to hospital. He was not in any pain, but could not eat much, which was distressing for a man who had always enjoyed his food, especially Ghanaian dishes. Jim came on a short visit which was a great joy. Unfortunately Winifred was having a tough time when she lost her unborn third child, and was unable to come.

The funeral took place at Wesley Church in Accra and was attended by about a thousand people. It was a lovely, dignified occasion, conducted by the President of the Methodist Conference the Right Reverend K. A. Dickson, supported by seven other ministers. There were so many tributes from people from all walks of life, but particularly the Ministry of Health and the Methodist Church. Afterwards the mourners were well-looked after both at Emmanuel Inn and Michael's own house at South Odorkor. The following Sunday we went to church again and back to Emmanuel Inn for some final funeral rites. At the request of Michael's family, I agreed to take part in a particular ancient ceremony which could have seemed strange and even frightening! But it was conducted in such a good-natured way that I felt quite relaxed.

A few days later, when I related this happening to a prominent Ghanaian lady doctor, she was horrified and told me that this ancient ceremony had been banned by law! I was taken aback to

Michael's grave with Henry, Karley, myself and Rosemary

think that I had broken the law again. Of course I knew that there were a lot of widow's rites that were abhorrent, and that the Church, and particularly the women, had been fighting hard to eradicate such obnoxious customs. What I had taken part in did not seem to fit into that category!

How can one describe the days and weeks after bereavement? I had been in the almost daily company of my spouse for more than forty-five years, and suddenly he wasn't there any more. How does one cope? Most of us go on to 'automatic pilot' for some considerable time. I continued to keep busy with my usual activities by day, and every night had a good weep into the pillow of my lonely bed.

Back to Ghana to Face Bereavement

I remember the first Christmas after Michael's passing, Karley and Kwesi whisked me off to their home in Cape Coast. We arrived just in time to tune in to the Service of Nine Lessons and Carols from King's College Cambridge, which Michael had enjoyed and never missed. Another day we took the boys swimming, and Kwesi persuaded me to don my swim suit and have a dip in the water - a soothing experience. One evening too we watched the funny film 'Mrs Doubtfire' and I laughed uproariously - the first time, I'm sure, for months. I went back to Accra determined to take each day and fill it with pleasant activities with family and friends. I considered myself lucky to have some of my children and grandchildren nearby, and cannot imagine what it would be like without their support and love.

I was also fortunate that, although retired, I had a second string to my bow - writing and editing books. Mr Sam Amarteifio had always encouraged me in this field. He himself had written successful novels such as 'Bediako the Adventurer' and 'The Forgotten Grandson' and sometimes I did proof-reading for him. My first attempt at producing a course in English Language for secondary schools never took off, but it kept me busy. I also abridged 'Watership Down' for young readers, but could not get permission from Richard Adams to publish it.

While I was waiting in England after Michael had gone ahead in 1994, I had heard some readings from John Bunyan's 'Pilgrim's Progress' on a BBC radio programme. Though the book is now old-fashioned and not to everyone's taste, I enjoyed it so much that I thought I would abridge it for Ghanaian readers - mainly junior secondary schoolchildren. I am not a creative writer but enjoy editing and abridging famous stories. I think I can claim to know what will appeal to Ghanaian readers.

I occupied myself with this while Michael was ill, and he enjoyed reading each chapter and making comments and corrections. He wrote a new tune for 'He who would valour see'. I love this tune although nothing can beat the well-known one by Vaughan Williams. So in the dreary days after Michael's passing, Mr Sam Amarteifio cheered me up by getting my abridged version of 'Pilgrim's Progress' published. A foreword was written by the Very Reverend Dr Jacob Stephens who had been one of the officiating ministers at Michael's funeral.

Later I was asked by Mr Sam-Woode, the publisher, to embark on some work for him. Strangely enough, he asked me to proof-read a book on widows' rites. Then I really found out what I had been spared, and felt thankful that Michael's family would not have allowed any of the unpleasant customs I read about while editing this book. I was belatedly thankful!

I was also asked by Mr Sam-Woode to write some reading books for young children. This really kept me busy, and I was lucky enough to have George Torgbor and later Ebenezer Acquah to draw the illustrations. We managed to complete 12 books - about 50 pages each with full-size pictures on every other page.

This activity was a real life-saver.

Living at South Odorkor, I had a few friends nearby whom I would visit and have a chat - Lovia, Mrs Chloe Dodoo and Peace Amarteifio as well as the lady living opposite, Mrs Yeboah. My friend the hairdresser was always ready to talk, as well as any passers-by I met on my way to buy a few things from 'The Jolly Spot'. In fact Ghanaians are never too busy to stop and talk, and I find this an endearing trait. In England, people are always in a great rush and I think they miss a lot as a result.

After a brief period when I felt too close to tears to go to church at all, I fell into the habit of going to the Ridge Church with Henry and Rachel, instead of to Wesley where the services were so long and where too many memories would resurface every Sunday.

As time went on I realised I had to come to some decision about whether to stay in Ghana for the rest of my life, or return to my roots in England. I made a visit to England in 1997 in order to try and resolve the problem. While I was there Winifred and Samuel's third daughter, Annabel, was born. I went to England again in 1999 when I helped Doreen celebrate her 75th birthday. I did not realise that I was seeing Tom for the last time. My daughter-in-law, Nancy, took me to see several flats in Reading run by sheltered accommodation housing associations, which would suit me well if I returned to England.

I was really finding it very difficult to decide. As I wrote in one of my circular letters, 'The pace of life is too fast in England, and too slow in Ghana; the poverty in Ghana is distressing, and so is the affluence in England (though neither may be within one's own circle); everything in England is planned far in advance, while everything in Ghana is "ad hoc" '. I also wrote, 'Whenever I take a piece of paper and try to award points for the advantages of living here or there, the added points give me 73 : 75 or 115 : 112 or something equally unhelpful.'

I was finding it increasingly difficult to cope with the heat and humidity in the tropics, and yet I didn't like the cold English weather. I had an air-conditioner but it was quite expensive paying for the electricity to have it on for more than a couple of hours a day. I had one solar panel that helped. Of course as soon as Michael died, his pension stopped. I now realised why, earlier on, my Ghanaian counterparts, wives of professional men, had been the wise ones pursuing their own careers with pensions.

In Ghana, I had the company of three of my children, Rosemary, Henry and Karley, whereas in England I would either settle in Dronfield and be close to Winifred and see little of Jim, or settle in Reading near Jim and see little of Winifred. One other thing was important - my increasing deafness! In Ghana, I found it difficult getting my hearing aids repaired, or even buying batteries. In England this would be no problem.

So my mind went back and forth. I did not want to make a hasty decision and regret it. Outside the house at South Odorkor grew a beautiful white bougainvillea. Usually they are pink, mauve or red and the white variety is rather special. We often used it as a background for photos, and I have one of myself standing in front of it. I sent a copy to a dear friend of mine in England. In her letter of thanks, she told me how she looked at it, and saw Michael standing beside me, and then in a flash the vision was gone. She even described what he was wearing. This gave me a warm feeling which I treasured.

Some time later, I had decided to have a kitchen made upstairs where the open back verandah was, immediately above the downstairs kitchen. It was quite a straightforward job and Rosemary was in charge. The workmen happened to come on May 20th, 2000 which would have been our golden wedding anniversary. While they were working, there was a sudden violent storm - rain pelting down, lightning flashing, thunder crashing, and a powerful wind sweeping down the alley between our house and our neighbour's, almost like a tornado.

The workmen hastily carried inside the cement they had been mixing outside. The storm subsided as quickly as it arose, and by the end of the day, the new kitchen was well on the way to completion. It wasn't until the next morning that I went outside. To my amazement, the beautiful white bougainvillea had been severed close to the ground and all its branches snapped off.

Usually when a bougainvillea has been cut down new shoots quickly appear and the bush revives, but this never happened in this case.

This simple incident just tipped the scales and, rightly or wrongly, I interpreted it as a sign that I should move on. I had asked for a sign and had got it - though I am the least 'mystical' person you could imagine!

Myself by the white bougainvillea bush

~ *Chapter 17* ~

Return to My Roots

Before I left Ghana, Karley had resigned from her post as Assistant Headmistress at Wesley Girls' High School, where she had been working for nearly twenty years. She then got a job as a Maths teacher at the Hermann Gmeiner International College at Tema. Kwesi had always been the one to drive the car everywhere, and Karley had only recently obtained her driving licence, so the move was quite difficult for her. At first she was lucky enough to be invited to stay with a family living close to the school. This was a temporary arrangement and, after that, she stayed with me at South Odorkor and travelled to Tema daily. This meant getting up exceedingly early. She didn't always have the car, and sometimes Mr Clottey, Henry's driver, took her in the morning, and she made her own way home in the afternoon. Coming home, she usually she got a lift with a friend to the centre of Accra, and then took a taxi to South Odorkor.

At this time, there was a spate of horrible murders taking place. Young women were whisked away (usually in a taxi) to a remote place where they were murdered, and the blood drained from their bodies. Most people assumed the blood was to be used for ritual purposes. I really didn't know whether to be more worried when she was driving herself, or when she had to take a taxi. You can imagine the agony of mind I went through when she was a little late!

At this time too, preparations were being made for further elections. Jerry Rawlings had served ten years as a military head of state, and then a further eight years as the democratically-elected President. Again to his credit, he agreed to step down in line with the constitution which states that the President cannot serve more than two elected four-year terms. This was a very exciting election, held in December 2000, with John Kufuor standing as leader of the New Patriotic Party (NPP), and John Atta Mills standing as the new National Democratic Congress (NDC) leader instead of Jerry Rawlings. Both were equally highly-respected intellectuals. There had to be a second 'run-off' election for president, and then Kufuor won by a clear majority. Even those who supported John Mills felt proud that history had been made because it was the first time since independence that the opposition had gained power through the ballot box, rather than by the power of the gun. Soon after the elections, the murders stopped. Was this a coincidence?

I finally arrived back in England on May 18th 2001. I had not told anyone in Ghana, except for Rosemary, Henry and Karley that I was thinking of settling in England permanently. I bought a single ticket but was quite prepared to go back if I failed to find suitable accommodation in England. Doreen's husband, Tom, had been gradually deteriorating in health, and had moved into a nursing home. A few months later he died, on May 14th, just before I left Ghana. On my arrival, I stayed a couple of nights with Jim and Nancy, before rushing down to Lymington to give Doreen as much support as possible in her bereavement. The funeral was on May 24th. Afterwards I stayed a week or two before going to stay with Winifred and Samuel and their three daughters.

About four months after Tom died, my younger brother, Peter, also died. I had been very close to him as a child, and then our paths took different directions. He did not take his studies seriously when he was at school, but after serving in the army, he had the opportunity of going to the Bath Academy of Art at Corsham. It was a great joy to us all, to see how he really found his true vocation at last. He had tried so many things, full-time and part-time - butchering, poultry-farming, drama - but nothing had lasted until now. He made an excellent teacher of art, and did well putting on his own exhibitions and selling many of his own

To Ghana with Love

My brother Peter

paintings.

This was after his marriage to Jenny Nightingale, a fellow student. They had four fine boys, Simon, Thomas, Barnaby and Lawrence. When in England, we visited them in their home in the lovely historic seaside town of Bosham (where King Canute's daughter is buried in the crypt of the church). After the boys grew up, Jenny took up printing, and also discovered her flair for writing short stories. She often sent them to me in Ghana and I enjoyed proof-reading them for her. She also sent me lots of CDs which I played on my computer while writing my books - my words flowed more smoothly with the type of music she favoured.

My sister Doreen

I was so pleased to be able to attend my brother's funeral. A sad occasion but full of thanksgiving for his happy marriage and successful career. Two years later my older half-brother Ken died, and it was equally sad yet satisfying to say a proper farewell, and meet up with that branch of the family.

This bereavement meant that only my older sister, Doreen, and myself are left of our generation. We were not particularly close as children, but now in our old age we find we have a lot in common. We rarely meet as she and her husband, Jim, live far away in Somerset, but enjoy phone calls, letters and cards. We are always exchanging news of children and grandchildren, and mention books we've read, or music we've listened to. They can boast of having a great grandson, living with his parents in Armenia! How the world has become one these days!

It took me six months of filling up forms and attending interviews before I was offered accommodation at Sutton Court in Reading. I had finally decided to settle there because the south was warmer, and most of my relatives and friends were in the south. It was also near Heathrow airport , and if my children (and grown-up grandchildren) were visiting or even passing through, they could easily drop in and see me. It is only Winifred who is far away, but easily reached by a direct train from Reading to Chesterfield or Sheffield.

I settled down in one of the many flats in this sheltered accommodation complex, which is very similar to Hallowes Court in Dronfield. It is very well run, and at the time, had a manager and his assistant living on the premises for any emergency. There was a social committee which organised outings, as well as concerts in the communal lounge, and regular tea-parties and buffet suppers. The building is very secure, and we all have our own front door. We can be as sociable or 'private' as suits each individual, but most of us quickly find a group of friends with the same interests. I soon joined Park United Reformed Church nearby, which is a friendly, lively church engaged in many activities.

As I update this edition, I have been back in England nearly eleven years, and it will soon be the sixteenth anniversary of

Myself in Reading

Michael's passing. I have never regretted my decision taken when the white bougainvillea was struck down! Family visitors come from Ghana and I must leave them to tell their own stories.

Some people think that the children of mixed marriages are bound to have problems, and that they find it difficult to know where they belong. In my experience, this is rarely the case. Instead, they have a double inheritance and their lives are enriched by having two countries and cultures to call their own. In addition they are able to act as bridges between their two countries, cultures and races. One only has to look at Barack Obama, the President of the United States of America, to see the benefits that this can bring to all sorts of people.

Looking back on my life, I cannot claim to have done anything extraordinary or outstanding. I have brought up a family, produced a few plays, and written a few simple children's books.

I sometimes like to recall a chapter I read in C. Northcote Parkinson's book 'East and West', where he paints a picture of the ideal British colonial ruler in India. Sometimes the European was a really admirable and talented person. Usually he was in good health, well-educated and had regular refreshing furloughs in England. This meant that during his tour of duty, he could be energetic and hardworking. He could travel to every corner of the small part of India that he was responsible for, and with his knowledge bring about many improvements, using the money and resources at his disposal.

Parkinson's extraordinary conclusion is that such marvellous people, though greatly to be admired, do a great deal of harm psychologically to the people they strive to help. Although he is talking about India, the same applies to countries in Africa or any other part of the world, where Europeans go to rule or to work, or to offer help through charities. These well-meaning expatriates leave the local people with a hopeless inferiority complex. They feel they are unequal to the foreigner in every way, and it is only the foreigner who can achieve anything and solve their problems. They begin to hate, not the foreigner, but themselves.

What an unprecedented point of view! But there's an element of truth in this and, rightly or wrongly, this view cheers me up! If one goes to a country less 'developed' (materially) than one's own, perhaps it is best to keep a low profile and make a modest contribution, rather than an outstanding one. But one thing I do regret - that I never learnt my husband's language. It would have been much easier to have drawn closer to my relatives if I had mastered the Ga language.

I am writing my story, modest as it is, for my family and descendents, whatever they are doing, and wherever they may be living in the world. I hope they all have much happiness in their lives. If it happens that tough experiences come along from time to time, I hope they will learn from Mark Tapley in Charles Dickens' 'Nicholas Nickleby'. He actually embraced hard times as an opportunity to show the strength of his character, and his ability to show his 'jolly disposition'. On one occasion he says to himself, 'Things are looking about as bad as they can look, young man. You'll not have such another opportunity for showing your jolly disposition, my fine fellow, as long as you live. And, therefore, Tapley, now's your time to come out strong; or Never!'

If my little story survives and is handed down through the years, I wonder what changes will have taken place in Ghana? Britain has made many changes in her culture and attitudes down through the years. There was a time when they believed in 'the divine right of kings', and when the aristocracy took the lion's share of the national wealth, building wonderful country houses while the lower classes lived in poverty. All that had to change. We also know of some horrible practices such as the burning of witches, and public executions.

No nation can stand still, and Ghana too has to cast off some of her negative attitudes, and aspects of her culture which try to hold her back. Then she can march forward after celebrating her fiftieth anniversary of independence. We might all give priority to different things that we need to aim for. My vote would go to a healthy work ethic, religious toleration, and the elimination of the PhD ('pull him down') syndrome.

Who knows but somebody might be reading my story when Ghana has become a great nation with a powerful influence in Africa, or even in the world. Why not? After all, Great Britain herself is a very small country - the same size as Ghana - and yet her achievements and influence have been - and still are - tremendous. Why should not Ghana be the same in the years to come?

The country is full of talented and intelligent people who are keen on training and education. At the same time they have always considered relationships with family and the community as important as money. Finally, they are mostly happy and cheerful people and, as any psychologist will tell you, these are the people who can be most creative and able to achieve their ambitions.

Michael and I

~ Appendix A ~

Herode Kpokpo

To Ghana with Love

Postscript

This book was written with the best of intentions, so please forgive any offence caused by what I have either included or omitted … certainly none is intended.

If anyone wishes to make comments, suggestions or criticisms, the author would be very pleased to receive them through the following email address:

ToGhanaWithLove@polytangle.com

www.polytangle.com